富豊

abundance

Finding the
American Dream in
a Japanese Kitchen

abundance

Finding the American Dream in a Japanese Kitchen 豊富

Taro Arai with L.G. Mansfield

Foreword by Nicholas Sparks

Book Design by Heidi Tomlinson
Photography by Jeremy Sykes

BLUE**FIG**
PUBLISHING

Book design by Heidi Tomlinson

Photography by Jeremy Sykes

Additional photography courtesy of:
The Arai family
Fulcrum Property (page 113)
Jayson Carpenter (page 4, 45)
Xsight Photography (page 46, 54)

Printed in China

ISBN: 978-0-615-38595-2

Library of Congress Control Number:
2010910125

Dedication

To my father, my grandfather, and our Heavenly Father

Acknowledgments

I am eternally grateful to my parents for filling my life with abundance, even at times when we had so little. I love you for everything you have taught me.

My brother, Nao, and my sister, Keiko, have been by my side throughout every step of this amazing journey. Thank you for being my best friends.

Haru, Mikuni's COO and my wonderful brother-in-law, is a driving force behind our success. Thank you for your wisdom. Yuka, my sister-in-law, is a joyous addition to the Arai family. I'm so happy that you are part of us.

My wife Machiko and my four children—Koki, Chiyoh, Kayji, and Chisay—are my inspiration every day. Nothing would be possible without you.

This project would never have gotten started without the invaluable advice and direction of chef Bob Blumer. Any time you want to cook side by side, I'll be there.

I am indebted to Nicholas Sparks for writing the foreword to this book. You have been a part of Mikuni since the very beginning, and I treasure our enduring friendship.

Without Elle Mansfield's determination to understand who I am and her talent in communicating my heart's message, this project could not have been accomplished. I am so grateful to you for guiding me through this process.

Before this project started, I had no idea how a book comes together. I now know the value of having a book designer, and I cannot imagine what it would have been like without Heidi Tomlinson's important contributions.

It was an amazing and fun experience for me to witness Jeremy Sykes's talent in photography—and on the golf course, too! I appreciate your contribution toward making this book unforgettable.

In its earliest days, Mikuni was blessed by the generosity of Dr. Yasuo Hara. I hope my gratitude reaches you wherever you are.

Mikuni's partners and investors are the foundation and the soul of our enterprise. My heartfelt gratitude to every one of you.

Our day-to-day operation is enriched by the expertise and vision of Mikuni's talented corporate team, including Derrick Fong, Jeanne Mabry, Kevin Kim, Raymond Ho, and Hiro Mitsuhashi. You have taken us to great heights of excellence and success.

Everything that Mikuni has become is due to the talent of our brilliant chefs and the commitment of our dedicated staff. Thank you for being part of our family.

I extend special thanks to my best friends—you know who you are—for your endless encouragement and support. Thank you for always steering me in the right direction.

Saving the most important for last, I thank our Mikuni guests for loyalty and support beyond measure. If it were not for your belief in us, there would be no story to tell.

Table of Contents

Nicholas Sparks with Taro Arai

Foreword

Horatio Alger.

I offer the name because it is often synonymous with what it means to achieve the "American Dream"—whatever that is. Horatio Alger (Jr., if you want to be specific) was an author who wrote (often heavily fictionalized) "rags-to-riches" stories. We all know exactly what that means: they were stories of some down-on-his-luck individual who, through will and perseverance and sometimes a bit of luck, eventually reaches the goals he's set for himself, dreams that had once seemed almost inconceivable.

I don't care what the critics say. I like Horatio Alger Jr. and all that his books implied might be possible. I find them inspiring. I appreciate the belief that someone, no matter where they came from, can somehow, through hard work, discipline, will, and perseverance, overcome all the odds and become a success.

Enter, of course, this particular book, and all the participants in it.

Let's rewind a bit, back to 1989. I want you to imagine a recent college graduate, newly married to the love of his life and as poor as a church mouse, as he heads into a small restaurant in the middle of a strip mall with his wife. Pat and Billy Mills, close friends of ours, had invited us to lunch at a place called Mikuni. I'd never heard of the restaurant, not surprising since it had only recently opened its doors, but we showed up expecting nothing memorable, except perhaps the chance at having a wonderful conversation. The restaurant, Pat and Billy explained as we parked the car, was "their little secret."

We were shown to our table by a delightful young lady. There were maybe six or eight tables total in the entire restaurant, but only two of them were occupied. The sushi bar could seat three or four; no one, however, was seated. At the sushi bar stood a young man with a broad, friendly smile and engaging personality who would cut and dice and roll the sushi items we ordered, if we ordered any of those items at all. He waved and smiled and said hello as we took our seats.

Our waiter arrived moments later. It was hard to tell his age other than that to think he was somewhere in his fifties, and he told us he was the proprietor. He noted that his wife and children comprised the staff, and after some further questioning, he explained that Mikuni means "kingdom of God" in Japanese. It turns out that he'd lived much of his life as a Christian minister in Japan, but had recently moved to the United States. Now, in addition to his continuing work as a Christian minister, he'd decided to open a restaurant. His wife, he told us, was a wonderful cook. On Sundays, he decided, he would continue to minister in a local church, but the restaurant would occupy the rest of his time. It was the family business, he said, and he had high hopes for the future.

We've all heard this story a million times, right? Immigrant moves to the country, and because his wife cooks well, the family decides to open a restaurant. Then, after years of struggle, the restaurant eventually ends up closing. It's not uncommon. Restaurants are a hard business. Ask around. As a general rule, the only way to make a small fortune in the restaurant business is to start with a large fortune.

Anyway, we ordered our food—including the salad bar and some sushi—from a young man. The owner brought our food and refilled our water glasses every time they'd dipped half an inch. It was obvious he wanted us to be pleased.

Long story short, the food was amazing. The presentation was beautiful. The salad bar was delicious, with exotic flavors and selections I'd never tried before. The sushi was dazzling, almost like art. And the taste...ask me now and I still can't pinpoint why it has always stood out in my mind, other than to say it was better. Not only when it comes to Japanese restaurants, but better as in any food I'd ever tasted.

High claims, I know. I don't know enough about the art of making food to give specific reasons as to why I felt that way. What I can tell you is that in the next three years while still living in Sacramento, I visited Mikuni probably forty times, and every time I went, the place grew even more crowded. The secret, it seemed, was getting out. With every visit, I realized that other people felt exactly the same way I did. When the business next door to the restaurant closed, Mikuni took over the space, doubling their occupancy limits, but it became harder and harder to get a table. The restaurant was always filled—and by that, I mean always. In time, they expanded again, then again, and still, the demand wasn't sated. Little by little, it seemed, Mikuni was taking over the strip mall.

The family opened a second restaurant, then a third, and the crowds continued to come. They opened even more restaurants. Now, years later, all of them continue to thrive. The food, if anything, has improved over time, something I never thought possible. And part of that reason, maybe one of the largest parts, is because of the man who looked too young to be handling a knife the first time I saw him. His name is Taro, and in many ways, we've grown through adulthood together. My wife and I knew him before we had children and long before I ever became a novelist. I knew him and his wife before they ever had children and before he became a world-class sushi chef. I consider him a friend, and I couldn't be happier for his, and his family's, success. It's fun for me to say, I knew him when...because in this case, quite frankly, it's true. I respect his ability and all that his family has done, so much so that I put the name of the restaurant—Mikuni—in my second novel, Message in a Bottle. Every time I visit Sacramento to visit my family—along with Pat and Billy Mills, of course—I always swing by Mikuni to eat and say hello to old friends and marvel at how well it's turned out for them.

Their story, in all the ways that count, is a story that Horatio Alger Jr. would have been proud to write.

Please, read the book. It's a terrific tale of hardship and stress, of perseverance and discipline, of dreams and hopes, of belief and faith, all held together by the love of family as they strive to live the American dream. It's a book that will leave you inspired for all the right reasons. And, of course, if you ever have the chance, stop by Mikuni. You won't be disappointed.

Nicholas Sparks

Firas Nassif, Taro Arai, Nicholas Sparks, and Micah Sparks

Introduction

To me, this book represents many things. From turning points in my life to silly stories that highlight the memories...from glimpses into the traditions of the past to wide-eyed anticipation of the future...it is filled with all that I hold dear and true. It is my greatest wish that you will draw something useful, or motivational, or simply good to eat from these pages.

I have chosen to share stories that have contributed to the person I am today. They show the appreciation I have for my culture and the gratitude I have for the many blessings in my life. Some of these tales may bring a smile to your face, others may make you thoughtful, and a few may leave you inspired. I've always said, "If I can do it, anyone can."

The recipes I have included are an invitation for you to explore the world of sushi-making and to taste how it has evolved over the years into a contemporary blend of eastern and western flavors. Feel free to experiment and substitute ingredients if you do not have easy access to some of the specialty Asian items. After all, the concept of evolution is to take something to the next level! Keep in mind that each roll will serve one person, but you'll have a lot more fun if you make several different types and share.

I invite you to try something new, to experiment, to dive into a cuisine I hold close to my heart. And if you should create a dish that's original, delicious, and exciting, please e-mail your discovery to me via my Web site: mikunisushi.com.

Tanoshinde kudasai ne! (Enjoy!)

Japanese Food Glossary

Alaskan king salmon: The largest and rarest of the Alaskan wild salmon, renowned for its rich flavor, tender meat, and high omega-3 content

Bigeye tuna: A smaller type of tuna distinguished by its large eyes, with firm, deep-red flesh, a low fat content, and rich flavor, called mebachi maguro in Japanese

Bluefin tuna: An extremely large tuna with deep-red flesh and a high oil content; rarer and more expensive than other types of tuna; called hon maguro in Japanese

Bonito: English word for the Japanese katsuo, a type of fish

Boston scallop: Large ocean shellfish commonly found in New England

Canadian albacore tuna: A delicately flavored fish found in the waters of the North Pacific

Copper River salmon: Silvery salmon with a bright red flesh, a firm texture, and a rich flavor; found in the Copper River in Alaska

Daikon: Long, white Japanese radish

Dashi: A basic soup stock made from dried fish and seaweed; used for miso soup and many different sauces

Garlic chips: Fresh garlic cloves that are thinly sliced, then deep-fried

Hamachi: Yellowtail imported from my home island of Amakusa in Japan

Kaiware: Daikon radish sprouts

Katsuo bushi: Dried bonito flakes

Kimchi: Pickled Korean vegetables with seasonings

Kombu: Kelp; seaweed

Kyushi hamachi: Yellowfin tuna

Maguro: Tuna, specifically the leaner flesh from the sides; called ahi in Hawaiian

Masago: Smelt roe; I call it orange pop rocks

Mirin: Sweetened rice wine (sake) used for cooking

Miso: Fermented bean paste, available in both white and red varieties; at Mikuni, we mix both varieties for our miso soup

Momiji oroshi: Dried ground Japanese chili peppers blended with grated daikon radish

Nigiri-zushi: Raw fish atop small mounds of vinegared rice; the initial "s" in "sushi" is changed to a "z" for easier pronunciation

Nori: Dried seaweed

Panko: Japanese bread crumbs

Rakkyo: Pickled Japanese shallot

Rayu: Chili oil

Sake: Rice wine; used for just about every type of cooking—and, of course, drinking

Salmon pearls: Large, orange-colored salmon roe; also recommended for fishing by Taro's bait shop

Sansho pepper: A ground berry from the Japanese prickly ash shrub with a sharp, mint-like flavor

Sashimi: Sliced raw fish

Shichimi togarashi: Japanese spice blend made of togarashi, sansho pepper, white sesame seeds, nori flakes, dried orange peel, black hemp seeds, and white poppy seeds

Shiso leaves: A mint-like herb also known as Japanese perilla and beefsteak plant; Japanese basil

Soybean wrap: A thin wrapper made from soybeans and used as a substitute for nori; also called mamenori

Sriracha sauce: A hot chili sauce

Sushi: Any dish made with vinegared rice

Sushi-grade: Fish that is suitable for eating raw because it has been frozen for seven days at negative-4 degrees Fahrenheit, or flash frozen for 15 hours at negative-31 degrees; not every type of fish must meet the freezing requirements

Tai: Red sea bream; called madai in Japanese; often served at New Year's and other festive occasions

Tasmanian ocean trout: A member of the Pacific Salmon family of trout; basically a cross between steelhead and rainbow trout

Tempura: Lightly battered and fried seafood or vegetables

Tenkasu: Tempura crumbs

Tobiko: Flying fish roe

Togarashi: Hot Japanese chili

Tonkatsu sauce: A Japanese sauce similar to Worcestershire sauce or steak sauce; I call it Japanese A1 sauce

Ume: A Japanese plum, sometimes referred to as a Japanese apricot

Wasabi: Japanese horseradish, traditionally grated into a green paste and used as a condiment for sushi and sashimi

Wheat paper: A wrapper made from wheat and used as a substitute for nori; I'm probably the only sushi chef who ever uses it, since it's far from traditional

Yellowfin tuna: A smaller species of tuna with a lighter-colored flesh, firm texture, and fairly high oil content

Yellowtail: A large marine fish that is a member of the jack family; related to pompano; called hamachi in Japanese

Yuzu: A highly prized and expensive citrus fruit, similar to a lemon or a tangerine

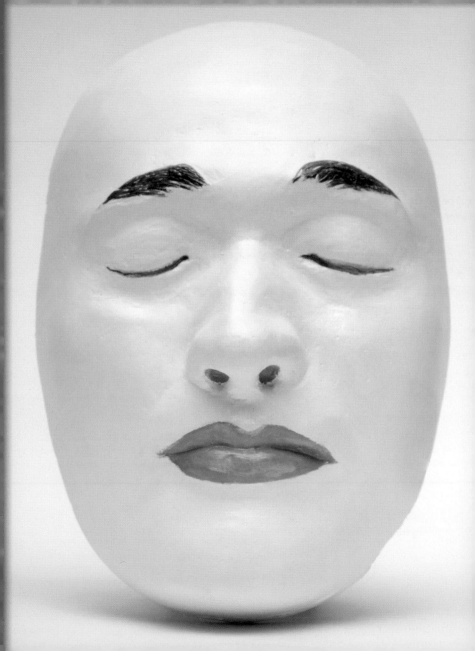

JAPANESE TRADITIONS

AND ETIQUETTE

豊富

FUN & FASCINATING

Food Facts

The kanji symbols for "sushi" can be translated three ways: vinegared rice, delicious fish, and happy meal.

The largest Pacific bigeye tuna, found in Cabo Blanco, Peru, weighed 435 pounds. The largest Atlantic bigeye tuna, found in Gran Canaria, Spain, weighed 392 pounds, 6 ounces.

In January of 2010, a giant bluefin tuna fetched 16.3 million yen ($177,000) in an auction at a wholesale fish market in Japan. The fish weighed 513 pounds and was the most expensive since 2001, when a 440-pound tuna sold for 20.2 million yen ($220,000).

The king salmon is the official fish of the state of Alaska.

Canadian albacore tuna is distinguished by pale pink flesh that turns off-white when it is cooked, making it the only species that can be labeled white meat tuna.

Every spring, the salmon returning to Alaska's Copper River must store extra fat and oils to survive the long journey. This additional fat makes them some of the tastiest fish in the world.

Tai, or red sea bream, is often given as a form of congratulations to the winners of sumo wrestling tournaments.

Tasmanian ocean trout has a milder and less salty flavor than Atlantic or farmed salmon.

Yellowfin tuna are very fast swimmers, and can maximize their speed by tucking their fins into special indentations in their bodies.

Shiso leaves are rich in carotene, vitamins B1, B2, B6, C, E, and K, and essential minerals such as calcium, iron, potassium, magnesium, and zinc. Renowned for their medicinal value, the leaves are used to treat asthma, coughs, colds, pain, and allergies. Shiso is an anti-inflammatory and an antibacterial, and is believed to help prevent food poisoning. A natural antiseptic, it is often used to treat eczema. In fact, my kids drink shiso tea whenever they have any kind of skin irritation, and it works!

Ume can be used to make umeboshi (pickled sour plum), which can last more than ten years. It can also be used to make umeshu (a type of sake), so it's the perfect fruit to have if you're stranded on a desert island. My mother has an ume tree in her yard, and we eagerly wait for the harvest season every year.

Japanese Traditions and Etiquette

Authentic Japanese cuisine is deeply rooted in a culture that emphasizes fresh, low-fat, wholesome eating, and the country's diet is considered one of the healthiest in the world. Rich in protein, vegetables, complex carbohydrates, and omega-3 fatty acids, a typical Japanese meal is heart-smart and extremely low in saturated and trans fats. Is it any wonder why the people of Japan live longer, healthier lives and have the lowest obesity rate in the developed world? In fact, Japanese people didn't start having problems with heart and weight until they began eating American fast food!

One of the healthiest Japanese foods is *natto*, fermented soybeans. My family and I eat this several times a week, and it is an excellent source of protein, vitamin B2, and vitamin K2. It also contains an enzyme called nattokinase, which is said to reduce and prevent blood clots. The benefits to the body are great...the taste is wonderful...but there are a couple of small problem: *natto* is very sticky and smells like old gym socks. If you can get past these stumbling blocks, I promise the nutritional values are worth it.

THE EVOLUTION OF SUSHI

The most traditional chefs rigorously follow the classic Japanese eating style, focusing on simple seasonings to allow the pure flavors of the food to shine through. More contemporary sushi masters are part of the sushi evolution, and they have made the transition to spicier, more elaborate fare. I, for one, love to experiment with new combinations of flavorings that often surprise my customers—and me! Since I eat sushi every day, I try to make different and interesting variations each time I prepare it.

Although I am untraditional in many ways, I embrace the classically Japanese belief that visual presentation is as important as taste and texture. The plates I use...the colors of the food...the way the components of a meal are assembled...all contribute to the complete dining experience.

THE SYMBOLISM OF FIVE

Japanese people believe that all five senses come into play when a meal is served: smelling an enticing aroma, tasting delicious food, seeing an artful arrangement on your plate, feeling different textures in your mouth, and hearing gentle background music (such as my *karaoke* singing) or the soft voices of your dining companions as you enjoy a meal together. Even the smooth warmth of a soup bowl, the coolness of a glass, or the delicate feel of chopsticks in your hand can enhance a meal's enjoyment.

Following this rule of five, I try to feature five tastes in the food I serve at my restaurants. While I'm sure you're familiar with salty, sweet, bitter, and sour, the Japanese recognize a fifth taste: *umami*. Literally translating to "flavor," it might be more accurately described with the words "savory," "meaty," or "rich."

I also have five basic methods when preparing food. One is *nama-mono*—raw—such as *nigiri-zushi* and *sashimi*. Another is *maki-mono*—rolled—such as Mikuni's famous Marilyn Monroll and Train Wreck. A third is *age-mono*—fried—such as shrimp tempura and deep-fried *gyoza*. Still another is *yaki-mono*—grilled—as in barbecued tuna and chicken *terayaki*. And the last is *mushi-mono*—steamed—such as rice and *shumai* (dumplings).

To me, presenting diners with a diversity of tastes and cooking methods opens them up to creative eating and offers endless possibilities. How boring it would be if we ate the same foods prepared the same way over and over again—life is way too short for that! Even though many of my regular patrons have their favorite dishes, I always try to introduce them to something new each time they dine with me.

Last but not least, I cannot finalize the symbolism of five without pointing out that the original Arai family that crossed the ocean from Japan to America numbered five. They are the source and the soul of Mikuni! In fact, we opened our first restaurant in May, the fifth month of the year.

FOOD CUSTOMS

A review of Japanese culinary traditions must include rice, since so much symbolism is attached to it. Rice is believed to have made its first appearance in Japan more than two thousand years ago, and for centuries it was available to only the wealthiest people and the most prestigious families. To everyone else it was a rare delicacy and a special treat—especially during wartime—so its consumption was limited to the most noteworthy occasions.

These days, rice is a staple in Japanese cooking. It is served with all meals at all times of the day—breakfast, lunch, and dinner—and is also used to make cakes, flour, vinegar, and wine. The most common rice is *hakumai*, white rice, which is polished to remove the outer portion. When we were kids, my dad made us eat *genmai*, brown rice, for its health benefits.

That brings us to a timeless beverage in Japan: sake, or rice wine. Pronounced "sock-ay" in Japan but commonly referred to as "sock-ee" in America, its origins date back two thousand years. It has long been looked upon as a drink to be shared with friends and family, and it is an important component of most meals.

Sake is available in many varieties—from flat to sparkling, from playfully fruity to seriously rice-like. From a production point of view, there are five basic types of sake and several less common ones. It can be served warm or chilled, in a squat cup or a tall glass. The alcohol content ranges from about 6 percent—common in the varieties that have been diluted with fruit juices—to about 20 percent. In traditional sake, the two main ingredients are rice and water, and it is brewed in a style more similar to beer-making than wine-making.

I'm a big fan of sake, because it's light and comparatively free of congeners—the toxic chemicals that form during fermentation and cause some nasty hangovers. Premium sake has no additives or preservatives, and all sake is sulfite free. My grandpa drank sake all his life, and he lived until his nineties. That's proof enough for me that sake—in moderation, of course—is good for you!

In my yearly visits back to Japan, I always make it a point to visit several sake breweries. There are about eighteen hundred of them throughout the country, and they produce about ten thousand different varieties. How wonderful it would be to get to sample every one of them before I leave this earth!

By the way, it is interesting to note that the Japanese word for "salmon" is also sake. To avoid confusion between the fish and the wine, we usually refer to the salmon as *shake* (pronounced "shock-ay") at the sushi bar.

THE WELL-BEHAVED DINER

Observing proper dining etiquette is of utmost importance in Japan. While many of the customs have not carried over into the American lifestyle, a few fundamental rules are worth noting.

Eating

When sharing a dish, take a bit of food from the platter and place it on your plate before eating it. This is considered common courtesy.

When eating *nigiri-zushi*, do not dip the rice side into your dish of soy sauce, since the liquid will cause the rice to fall apart. Instead, carefully turn the piece upside-down and dip the fish side. Leaving even a single grain of rice in the soy sauce is considered bad manners. It is perfectly acceptable to eat *nigiri-zushi* either with chopsticks or with your fingers.

When dining at a traditional sushi bar in Japan, it's likely that you will not be served *wasabi*. The local chefs believe they know exactly how much of this spicy condiment to put on each different type of sushi, and it is considered rude to ask for more. Fortunately, that's not the case in America. If you choose to, you can eat *wasabi* like guacamole!

A spoonful of rice left in the bottom of your bowl indicates a desire for more. This was never a common practice at our home when I was growing up, since we were too poor to bother with learning all those rules.

Even though slices of a sushi roll are often large, try to place the entire piece in your mouth, since eating it whole will allow you to enjoy all the flavors at once. If a piece is simply too big, you have my permission to cut it with your chopsticks or bite into it. Just be warned that less expensive types of *nori*, the dried seaweed commonly used to make rolls, can be difficult to tear apart with your teeth. (Of course, we never use this kind at Mikuni!) If you run into a problem, just relax and don't worry if you make a bit of a mess. In my book, enjoying your food is more important than being tidy.

Large pieces of food, such as fish and *tempura*, may be cut into bite-sized pieces with chopsticks. This may take a bit of practice, since chopsticks certainly don't have the cutting power of a knife. But since Japanese food is usually fairly soft, you'll eventually get the knack of it.

When eating soup, it is proper to lift the bowl and sip. Slurp just a bit if you must, but remember that, in Japan, it is more acceptable to make slurping noises when eating noodles.

Using Chopsticks

When taking food from a platter, reverse the chopsticks so you reach with the end that does not go into your mouth. Again, this is a show of respect for your fellow diners.

When your chopsticks are not in use, place them beside your plate—parallel, not crossed—or on a chopsticks rest, if one is provided. Do not place them across the top of your bowl.

Do not skewer food with your chopsticks, and never leave them standing up in your food. In Japan, this is called a "cemetery," and it is a practice that is definitely frowned upon.

If you are served wooden chopsticks in a restaurant, it is fine to remove the tiny splinters by gently rubbing them together. Do not, however, make a big show of doing so, since it indicates that you believe the utensils are cheap. (They are, of course, but there's no need to point this out to your waiter or the sushi chef!) Also keep in mind that disposable chopsticks are far more hygienic than reusable ones.

Drinking

It is considered impolite to pour your own drink. Whether consuming sake or tea, it is proper to pour your companion's drink and allow your companion to pour yours.

Leave your glass or cup full if you do not want anything more to drink. An empty glass means you would like a refill.

Japanese Food-Related Phrases

If you practice these phrases, it might be fun to use them the next time you dine in a Japanese restaurant.

Konnichiwa *[kon-nee-chee-WAH]*—"Hello."

Itadakimasu *[ee-tah-DAH-kee-mahss]*—Literally means "I humbly receive," and can be loosely translated to "Let's eat." Customary to say at the beginning of a meal.

Gochisosama-deshita *[go-CHI-so-sa-ma de-SHI-ta]*—Literally, "I was spoiled," but essentially means "Thank you for the meal." Customary to say upon finishing a meal.

Oishii desu *[o-I-shi DE-su]*—"This is delicious."

Sugoi *[soo-GOY]*—"Wonderful."

Cho-sugoi *[cho soo-GOY]*—"Super wonderful."

Ichiban *[EE-che-ban]*—"Number one."

Omakase *[oh-ma-kah-SEH]*—"It's up to you." Said when you're leaving the choice of food up to the chef.

Oaiso dozo *[oh-EYE-so DOH-zoh]*—"Check, please." (When slurred, can sound a lot like, "Why so much?")

Onegai shimasu *[oh-neh-gigh shee-MOSS]*—"Please."

Arigato *[ah-ree-GAH-toh]*—"Thank you."

Sayonara *[sigh-oh-NAH-rah]*—"Goodbye."

Taro *[TAH roh]*—First son; **Arai** *[ah-RYE]*—Wild. That makes me the original wild child!

豊富

THE ART OF SUSHIOLOGY

You may have wondered about the person who first pulled a wriggling fish out of the ocean, cut it open, and decided to eat it raw. Was he too lazy to roast it over an open flame? Was he so hungry that he couldn't wait to get a fire going? Did he not know how to start a fire? Or did he just take a leap of faith and sample a bite out of curiosity? Whatever the reason, I'm glad he decided to try something different, and I'm grateful for the discovery of this fine cuisine.

These days, we think of sushi as a raw-fish delicacy, but that's not actually the case. Technically, sashimi is raw fish, while sushi means "vinegared rice." In fact, depending upon how you interpret the kanji symbols that make up the word "sushi," it can also translate to "delicious fish" or "happy meal"—my personal preference. If you've spent much time in Japanese restaurants, you know that sushi isn't necessarily raw at all, since many rolls and *nigiri-zushi* are made with cooked foods, such as shellfish, eggs, seared tuna, and eel.

The exact history of sushi is unclear, and claims of its origin date back as early as the 5th century B.C. It is a commonly held belief that it did not originate in Japan, but likely got its start in Southeast Asia or China. I've always concluded that Jesus was the first sushi chef, since He managed to feed five thousand of his disciples with two fishes—and the Bible doesn't mention anything about cooking it.

In its earliest form, sushi consisted of salted fish wrapped in fermented rice, which was a way of preserving the fish for future consumption. It was left to sit for a period of a few months to a few years, then the rice (which was pretty offensive by then) was discarded and the fish was eaten. Sometimes customers will ask me for traditional sushi, and I tell them I'll start making it right away and they can return in four or five years when it's ready.

TYPES OF NIGIRI-ZUSHI AND ROLLS

There are many different ways to prepare sushi. Of course, I suggest you try them all so you can choose your favorites. Let's take a look at the possibilities.

Nigiri-zushi—also called a finger roll—is made with sushi rice on the bottom and fresh fish or other ingredients on the top. It is oval-shaped and hand-pressed, and may include a strip of *nori* and a dab of *wasabi*. It is the most internationally common style of sushi.

Maki is the Japanese word for "roll," and the term *maki-zushi* includes a variety of sushi that is rolled in *nori*. Examples of this style are *hoso-maki*, a basic roll that usually contains just one filling. Options include *kappa-maki* (cucumber) and *tekka-maki* (raw tuna).

Futo-maki is a large, thick roll that features several ingredients. This is where chefs get to be really creative, because they can play with different flavors and textures to create a dish that is both tasty and artful. *Futo-maki* was originally created as picnic food, because it's a great way to combine variety with portability.

Ura-maki goes against the grain by placing the rice on the outside of the roll. The rice surrounds a layer of *nori,* which encases the filling, and the top is often sprinkled with sesame seeds or *tobiko*. This is one of the most popular rolls among Mikuni diners, since they can choose to add fish, sauce, or anything else on top of the roll. A California roll is a classic example of *ura-maki*.

If you're the kind of sushi lover who wants to get to the food quickly and easily and prefers something larger than a finger roll, you might become a fan of *temaki*, a hand roll. It consists of a cone-shaped piece of *nori* filled with a diversity of ingredients—the perfect grab-and-go meal.

Chirashi-zushi, which translates to "scattered sushi," refers to a bowl filled with sushi rice and other ingredients, including an assortment of vegetables. My mother maintains a *chirashi* garden just so she can make this favorite dish as often as possible. There's nothing fresher!

IT'S ALL ABOUT THE RICE

Rice is a very important part of the Japanese culture, and it is the key ingredient to great sushi. Learning how to make perfect sushi rice is a long and difficult process, and any successful Japanese chef will tell you that it requires at least five years of training. Imagine—more than five years to master the preparation of just one item of food! That's just too long for me, so I've figured out a way to teach it to the Mikuni chefs in about five days. This gives all of us more time to enjoy the sushi we make!

Many factors come into play when preparing the rice, including freshness, humidity, temperature, and altitude. When we opened our Mikuni restaurants in Lake Tahoe and in the Mile High City of Denver, the recipes had to be readjusted for each area's increased elevation.

The ideal sushi rice has a consistency that is sticky enough to hold together, but not so sticky that the first bite glues your mouth shut. That would make it impossible to eat more sushi, and who wants to go hungry? To learn how to make perfect sushi rice, see the recipe on page 41.

How to Make a Sushi Roll

Step 1

Step 2

Step 3

Step 4

Step 5

Step 6

Step 7

Step 8

Step 9

Step 10

Step 11

Step 12

Step 13

Step 14

Step 15

A rainbow roll is a classic example of a simple inside-out roll. Here's how to make it:

Step 1. Place a sheet of nori shiny-side-down on a bamboo mat.

Step 2. Place 4½ ounces of sushi rice on top of the nori, spreading it evenly with your fingertips.

Step 3. Carefully flip it over so the nori side is up and the rice side is down.

Step 4. Add inside ingredients—in this case, some crab.

Step 5. Using the edge of the mat as a guide, start rolling away from you, applying gentle pressure and shaping the roll as you go.

Step 6. Lift the mat.

Step 7. Tuck in any ingredients that may have gone astray.

Step 8. Continue to roll completely.

Step 9. Place your fish of choice on top of the roll.

Step 10. Cover the entire roll with plastic wrap.

Step 11. Using a sharp knife, cut through the roll.

Step 12. Use the mat to re-form the roll and make it as neat as possible.

Step 13. Remove the plastic wrap.

Step 14. Arrange the roll on a serving plate.

Step 15. Garnish with *tobiko* and thinly sliced green onions.

HOW TO SELECT FISH

Most of Mikuni's fish comes from the Tsukiji fish market in Japan. When shopping for fish locally, I look for the following clues to indicate its freshness:

- **Smell**—The aroma of fresh fish bring me back to the beautiful ocean. Old or bad fish has a strong fishy odor reminiscent of a bait shop.
- **Eyes**—The eyes of the fish should be clear, bright, and plump. If the pupils are cloudy, the fish is not fresh.
- **Gills**—These should be red. If they are turning black and appear either slimy or dry, walk away.
- **Color**—Look for flesh that is bright and lustrous.
- **Consistency**—The flesh of the fish should be firm and elastic. Don't be afraid to give it a poke in the market to make sure it's not mushy.

THE BEST SUSHI KNIVES

A knife for a sushi chef is like a sword for a samurai. In fact, traditional sushi knives are usually made from high carbon steel, which is also used to forge samurai swords. A good knife can cost a small fortune—I paid close to three thousand dollars for one of mine! The more expensive a knife is, the greater the sharpness and the longer it will last, so I recommend buying the best one you can afford. Then be sure to keep it in good condition, with a clean, sharp cutting edge.

The design of a sushi knife is uniquely different. It is honed to a razor-sharp edge on only one side of the blade, allowing for the cleanest possible cut—an important factor when slicing delicate, raw fish. Each specific job has its own particular knife, and the most popular ones are as follows:

- **Yanagi**—A long, slender knife with a willow-leaf blade and a pointed end; used for slicing sashimi
- **Deba**—A wide, heavy cleaver; used for cutting fish
- **Gyutoh**—A thin and lightweight all-purpose tool similar to a Western chef knife; used for cutting rolls

HOW TO SLICE FISH

There are several basic cutting techniques, but the most commonly used ones are an angled cut and a straight cut. The thickness of the slice depends of the type of fish. For example, white fish is sliced more thinly than tuna, since tuna flesh is more likely to break apart if sliced too thinly. When cutting fish for sushi and sashimi, the flesh should be sliced against the grain for the best texture, taste, and appearance.

Instructions for an Angled Cut
Using a block of fish about the size of your hand, place it horizontally on a cutting board. Slice off a triangular piece to create an angled edge, and continue to cut following this angle, pulling the slice toward you.

Instructions for a Straight Cut
Place a block of fish horizontally on a cutting board. Make sure it has a squared-off edge. Position the knife at a 90-degree angle and slice straight down.

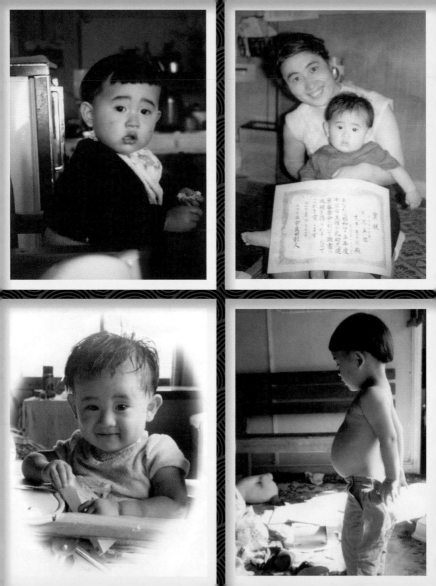

CHAPTER **1**

GROWING UP IN JAPAN

 "So don't worry about
these things, saying,
'What will we eat?
What will we drink?
What will we wear?'
These things dominate
the thoughts of
unbelievers, but your
heavenly Father already
knows all your needs.
See the Kingdom of
God above all else, and
live righteously, and He
will give you everything
you need."

—*Matthew 6:31-33*

There is an archipelago off the west coast of Kumamoto in Japan—a cluster of more than one hundred islands in the Amakusa Sea. The terrain is rough and mountainous, so it's not a very friendly place for farming. In fact, there aren't many industries on the islands at all. The people who live on Amakusa are mostly involved in forestry, growing oranges, and fishing. This rather primitive little place is where I was born.

My father, Koki, was the pastor of a Christian church on our island. A kind and compassionate man, he did his work for what it brought to his heart, not to his bank account. He was quick to share what little we had with anyone in need, so our family—my mother, Komichi; my brother, Nao; my sister, Keiko; and I—struggled financially during most of my childhood. As a baby, I often went without milk because my parents couldn't afford it. My father was able to provide only $150 each month to feed the family, and that little amount also had to cover the troubled individuals he frequently took in. The members of his church frequently helped us with donations of rice and vegetables, but there never seemed to be enough food.

In our attempt to become self-sufficient, we began to grow and raise our own provisions. My mother always loved to garden, so she turned her passion to planting and tending vegetables. My siblings and I raised chickens, enabling us to have eggs and fresh meat. The chickens also helped with fishing, because we would search for worms under their waste and use them as bait. Whatever we caught that day was dinner that night, which meant plenty of sashimi. After dinner, we would feed the fish bones to the chickens, continuing the life cycle that taught me a great deal about survival.

Fishing began at an early age for me, and it was as enjoyable to me as it was essential. My route to school included crossing a bridge, and I would set up my fishing net each morning, then check it on my way home to see what I'd caught. It wasn't long before I was skilled at cleaning fish, shucking oysters, and shelling crab and shrimp. I learned how to make the most of the resources that were available to me, relying on the little island to help keep my family fed.

LESSONS FROM MY FATHER

In our leisure time, my family loved to hike the mountains. A few times a month, we ventured off to explore our country. We would eat the fruit that grew along the way and we learned how to catch a variety of insects—my two favorite things to do while hiking.

When I was ten years old, we took a seven-hour hike up Mount Fuji. When we arrived at the top, we sat down to reflect on the beauty and grandeur that surrounded us. After a while, my father said it was time to head back. Halfway down the mountain, I realized I had left my backpack at the top. My father told me I had to retrieve it, and all I could focus on was the time and energy it would take to hike back up. I was not a happy kid.

What I didn't realize at the time was the character that such a task was building. My dad taught my siblings and me how to dedicate ourselves to what we believe. By example, he showed us that challenging ourselves creates a strong work ethic that is necessary to achieve any goal. Although we didn't have much money, we had abundant love and amazing parents who demonstrated that having heart means having everything.

SHARING...LEARNING...DREAMING

When I was growing up, our house was always filled with people. My dad was a collector of children who had mental and emotional problems, and I often shared a room with them. Most of these kids had parents who had lost patience or heart, so we welcomed them into our family and treated them as if they were a part of us. And over time, they became just that. I learned a great deal about life from my roommates, particularly that we should be grateful for everything God blesses us with. I watched these kids struggle with some of life's simplest tasks, and it reminded me never to take anything for granted.

Needless to say, my childhood was far from ordinary. In addition to a houseful of people, we also had a zooful of animals—turtles, birds, cats, dogs (my favorite was a bulldog), chickens, and fish. At my uncle's place, which was located nearby, there were horses, cows, peacocks, pigs, and rabbits. You name it, and I grew up around it. But I was the wildest animal of all!

With so many people in our household and our constant shortage of funds, I never ate out when I lived on Amakusa. In fact, I didn't have the opportunity to taste a hamburger, steak, or hot dog until I moved to the United States. I had never been to a sushi bar either, because sushi has always been an expensive luxury in Japan. Sure, I had plenty of homemade sashimi made with the fish we caught, but I had never experienced the added dimension of having food prepared by a professional chef.

I had sushi for the first time when I was fifteen, and I started off with the most basic roll—a kappa maki, or cucumber roll. My dad ordered it for me, and it was love at first bite. Just as I was about to ask if I could try something else, my dad asked for the check. This simple taste was all he could afford, but it represented the beginning of something very important to me.

Dining at the sushi bar was my dream when I was small, and that's where it all began: a little kid...on a tiny island...with a dream as large as life.

american dream roll

Named for my strong desire to move to America

1 sheet nori (dried seaweed)

1½ ounces sushi-grade wild Copper River salmon, raw

1½ ounces sushi-grade Bluefin tuna, raw

2 panko-fried shrimp*

¼ avocado, sliced

1 ounce snow crab legs, cooked

vegetable oil, enough for deep-frying

tempura batter (recipe at right)

American Dream Sauce (recipe at right)

1 green onion, thinly sliced

Prepare the roll following the instructions on page 26. Start with a sheet of nori, and top it with a layer of salmon, a layer of tuna, panko-fried shrimp, avocado, and snow crab legs. Roll up.

Heat vegetable oil in a deep pan to 350 degrees. Lightly dip the entire roll in tempura batter, then transfer to a deep-fryer basket. Submerge the roll in the hot oil and fry until crisp and golden. The ingredients inside the roll should not be cooked through. Remove carefully and drain on a rack. When cool enough to handle, slice into bite-sized pieces, pressing down firmly on both ends to settle the filling.

Spoon American Dream Sauce onto a serving plate, and place the pieces of the roll on top. Garnish with sliced green onion.

TEMPURA BATTER

1 pasteurized egg

1 cup ice water

1 cup all-purpose flour, sifted

In a small bowl, lightly beat the egg with chopsticks or a fork. Add ice water and flour, mixing just until blended.
(Alternatively, you can buy tempura mix at an Asian market and follow package directions.)

AMERICAN DREAM SAUCE

1 pasteurized egg yolk

¼ teaspoon sea salt

1 teaspoon rice vinegar

white pepper to taste

½ cup vegetable oil

½ teaspoon soy sauce

¾ teaspoon sesame oil

¼ cup ketchup

¼ cup Korean or Thai chili paste

In a small bowl, whisk the egg yolk with sea salt, rice vinegar, and white pepper. Add the vegetable oil a little at a time, stirring constantly. Add soy sauce, sesame oil, ketchup, and chili paste, and continue to whisk until well blended.

* Available at Asian markets. Alternatively, dip raw shrimp in beaten egg, then dip in panko (Japanese breadcrumbs) and deep fry until golden.

CHAPTER **2**

CULTURE CLASH

 "If a man is not
faithful to his own
individuality, he
cannot be loyal to
anything."

—Claude McKay,
Jamaican writer and
poet

Japanese people are famous for practicing the three Ps: politeness, punctuality, and patience. In spite of my heritage—and much to the dismay of my family—I have never possessed any of those qualities. Instead, I have always been famous for the three Fs: free, fun-loving, and freaky.

Even when I was a small child, I had a strong desire simply to be me, regardless of the shape my individuality took. In Japan, that kind of bold independence flies in the face of tradition. The country's culture stresses the importance of obeying the rules and doing precisely what is expected at all times, but despite my best intentions, I had a tough time staying on the path I was supposed to follow. Because of my individuality, what could a future in Japan possibly hold for me?

As I grew, my belief in freedom of expression grew right along with me. It seemed only fair that I should be free to express myself—that I should be able to say and do whatever comes naturally—but that is against the Japanese custom. My people have a saying, "If the nail comes up, hit it down," and I lived my early life as that nail. Every time I popped up with a new or different idea, I was brought down by the standards of the Japanese way. It's no wonder that by the age of ten, I was beginning to fantasize about a life outside of Japan.

GOING AGAINST THE GRAIN

My struggles with Japanese culture expanded into the school system, as well. From the very beginning, I tested the water nearly all the time. It wasn't that I was a bad kid—it's just that I had my own way of doing things. I found the Japanese approach to life to be much too serious, and I preferred being an independent thinker and having fun. Given the enormous difference between what I was supposed to do and what I wanted to do, I was in for an interesting childhood.

One of my earliest school memories is of an incident that happened in third grade. My teacher had instructed me to clean the floor of the classroom, which was a task every child was required to perform. I did what I was told, but I didn't do it in the proper way. Instead of using my hands, I lay down on my back and maneuvered the cleaning cloth with my feet. I was so caught up in fooling around that I didn't realize the vice principal had entered the room. In fact, I wasn't aware of his presence until I saw his shoes on the floor beside me. *Shimatta! (I'm busted)!*

I gazed up at his face, which seemed miles away from my spot on the floor, and I could see that he wasn't happy. I waited for him to yell at me, but he didn't say a word. Instead, he reared his foot back and kicked me. My emotions went from shock to anger to fear in seconds. Before I realized what I was doing, I grabbed his leg as he pulled back to kick me a second time. He fell to the floor—hard—and broke his arm. That incident set the tone for how my school years would continue.

My reputation as a difficult kid soon became widespread, and I became known among the school staff as the boy who marched to the beat of a different drum. Teachers and administrators alike knew my name, and they probably had my parents' phone number memorized. If there was a problem anywhere in school, odds are I was at the heart of it.

When I was in sixth grade, my teacher begged me not to attend class because I was such a distraction. My dad agreed to let me stay home, and I was perfectly happy to spend my time fishing and working around the house. After a month, the principal asked that I return, so that was the end of my independence. I went back to class, and all the discipline problems started up all over again.

I found the Japanese approach to life to be much too serious, and I preferred being an independent thinker and having fun.

FASHION STATEMENT GONE WRONG

So there I was—my independent flag flying at all times. I drove the school administrators crazy by bending the rules, and I made things worse by insisting on expressing my unique style.

For example, those of us who played sports were expected to shave our heads. Instead, I would try many different hairstyles—from shaving just one side of my head to sporting a reverse Mohawk. I enjoyed expressing myself in these unusual ways, and I liked standing out from the crowd. Unfortunately, it didn't serve me very well.

When I was about to start junior high, I ran into a problem. It was mandatory for male students to wear a black jacket and pants, a white collared shirt, a black hat, white socks, and white shoes with a yellow stripe. My older cousin gave me the entire outfit—except for the shoes. Because money was always tight in our family, I shopped around for the cheapest pair I could find. I ended up with white shoes with a red stripe, because they cost less than the ones with the requisite yellow stripe. Big mistake!

I showed up at morning assembly on the first day of school wearing my nice new shoes with the snazzy red trim. Unexpectedly, my teacher called me up to the front of the entire student body, which numbered about 2500 kids. I proudly walked up as though about to received an award of recognition, but instead, he smacked me across the face. "That," he said, "is what happens when you don't obey the rules!" My nose instantly gushed blood all over my white shirt—a perfect match to the rule-breaking red stripe on my footwear.

From my outfits to my attitude to the way I wore my hair—none of it fit into the Japanese way of life.

TIME TO MOVE ON

Although I wasn't even in my teens, I was old enough to realize that my personality was in direct contrast to the customs of Japan. I understood that freedom of choice was welcomed in the United States, and I constantly thought about a life there. I knew it would take hard work and a considerable amount of money to achieve my American dream, but I was determined.

I was eleven when I started working. I managed to land a newspaper route, and I had to get up at five o'clock in the morning, regardless of the weather, to deliver papers seven days a week, 365 days a year. Some mornings, my hands and face were so cold that I thought they would turn to ice. I was miserable, but I had a purpose and that kept me going. My parents rewarded me by giving me my first ever Christmas present: a pair of gloves. I cried when they gave them to me, because I knew I would be warmer and my job would be a bit easier. But more important, the gift meant that my mom and dad were supporting me in my dream of a future where I could be me. To this day, I have kept those gloves.

I took great pride in my paper route, and I always made sure the paper was as close as possible to each front door. After all, I *was* capable of sticking to the rules when I wanted something. The best part of the job was getting paid at the end of the month, and watching my profits increase was a constant reminder that I was closer to my dream. After five years, I managed to save six thousand dollars. It was finally time to leave Japan and set out to conquer America.

With my hard-earned savings, I bought airline tickets for my entire family, and on April 2, 1985, we landed at San Francisco International Airport. I remember the day as if it were yesterday, and my family still celebrates it every year as if it were a rite of passage. And I guess, in many ways, it was.

At last—I had arrived at the place where I felt my freedom lived. The opportunity for change and growth felt like an electrical charge, and the prospect of exploring this new side of the world thrilled me. I was both excited and overwhelmed as I realized that my life would never again be the same.

America the beautiful...home of the brave and the free...*my* home.

stop, drop and roll

Named for the fiery flavors of this spicy roll

½ sheet nori (dried seaweed)

4½ ounces sushi rice (recipe at right)

3 ounces sushi-grade Bigeye tuna, raw

½ ounce cucumber, peeled and sliced vertically into 2-inch strips

Spicy Freedom Sauce (recipe below)

1 small jalapeño, seeded and thinly sliced

shichimi togarashi (Japanese spice blend) to taste*

sriracha sauce to taste*

Prepare the roll following the instructions on page 26. Start with a sheet of nori, and top it with sushi rice. Chop half the tuna (1½ ounces) with sriracha sauce, and spread it on top of the rice. Add sliced cucumber. Roll up. Top the roll with remaining 1½ ounces of tuna.

Using a sharp knife, cut the roll into bite-sized pieces. Transfer to a serving plate.

Drizzle the roll with Spicy Freedom Sauce, top with jalapeño slices, and sprinkle with shichimi togarashi.

SPICY FREEDOM SAUCE

1 teaspoon kimchi (pickled Korean vegetables) juice*

1 teaspoon lime juice

2 tablespoons sriracha sauce (hot sauce)*

¼ teaspoon fresh ginger, minced

¼ teaspoon fresh garlic, minced

¼ teaspoon sesame oil

In a small bowl, whisk all ingredients until well blended.

Available at Asian markets

SUSHI RICE

The basic rice-to-vinegar ratio is 1 cup of vinegar for every 6 cups of uncooked rice.

1 cup short-grain white rice—Japanese-style rice

(At Mikuni, we use musenmai rice; look for pre-washed rice to save water and labor.)

1¼ cups water (Depending on the season, it may be necessary to adjust the water a bit. Newly harvested rice requires less water

1 (2-inch-square) piece kombu (dried kelp)*

2 tablespoons rice vinegar

1 tablespoon white sugar

½ teaspoon salt

Rinse the rice in a strainer or colander under cold running water until the water runs clear. Drain well. Place in a medium saucepan with 1¼ cups water and kombu. Bring to a boil, reduce heat to low, cover, and cook for 20 minutes until water is absorbed and rice is tender. Set aside. (Alternatively, prepare in an automatic rice cooker per manufacturer's directions, which is what we do at our restaurants. I highly recommend this method, because it is very advanced, useful, and incredibly easy.)

In a small saucepan, combine rice vinegar, sugar, and salt. Stir over medium-low heat until sugar dissolves. Poor mixture over rice until well coated. Slowly pour the vinegar mixture over the rice, and gently separate the grains by slicing a rice paddle across the rice rather than stirring. Use a hand-held fan to cool the rice as it absorbs the vinegar mix. This will produce a glossy finish. Do not refrigerate. Continue to cool at room temperature. Rice will dry as it cools.

NOTE: The recipe for sushi rice varies from restaurant to restaurant, from region to region. Once you've mastered the basic recipe, I encourage you to experiment with your own variations, such as apple cider vinegar, red wine vinegar, and other creative ingredients. And if you'd rather leave the labor to someone else, you can buy vinegar mix at any Asian market.

CHAPTER **3**

ADAPTING TO AMERICA

 "America lives in
the heart of every
man everywhere
who wishes to find
a region where he
will be free to work
out his destiny as he
chooses."

*Woodrow Wilson,
28th President of the
United States*

In spite of my passion for wanting to live in America, making the transition to a new culture did not come easily. For starters, the language posed a real problem for me, resulting in a lot of confusion.

Immediately upon arrival at San Francisco Airport, I was approached by a tall, African-American man—the first dark-skinned person I'd ever seen in my life—who greeted me with an enthusiastic "What's up?" I asked my dad to translate, since his English was more fluent than mine. When he told me what the man had said, I turned back to my new friend and happily replied, "Sky!"

The size of things in America also baffled me. On the way from San Francisco to Sacramento, we stopped at a fast-food restaurant where I had my very first hamburger. It was humongous! I soon came to realize that everything in the United States—from burgers and people to houses and freeways—is bigger, wider, longer, or taller. In fact, the only small thing was our church, the First Japanese Baptist Church in Sacramento, where my dad was asked to be the Japanese-speaking pastor.

For a mere four hundred dollars per month, my father took great pride in leading a ministry for a few dozen Japanese *issei* (first generation) parishioners, who were all in their nineties and beyond. It was nearly impossible to pay our rent and other living expenses on such a modest salary—until the church moderator stepped in.

Touched by my family's plight, this generous man wrote us a check for a thousand dollars. There were no strings attached, and his gesture was driven purely by kindness. To us, the money was worth a million dollars, and I vowed then that I would always try to help those less fortunate whenever I could.

THE GIANT TANGERINE

Getting from place to place in Sacramento always posed a problem, since there wasn't an extensive public transportation system like there is in Japan. My dad finally bought a used car for three hundred dollars, and although my family was excited at the prospect of having our own vehicle, we were shocked when we saw what it was.

There in the driveway, competing with the brilliant sunlight, sat a bright-orange convertible that had seen better days. It had only two seats for our family of five, and the door on the passenger side didn't open. But it was transportation, so we dutifully piled in and headed to our jobs at a local Japanese restaurant.

PAPERS AND PAYMENTS AND DOGS, OH MY!

Even though we were all working, our financial struggles continued. My dad had always been devoted to giving all he could—physically and financially—to his parish. Considering the amount of money he was giving away, we looked for ways to bring in more funds. Since my newspaper route in Japan was lucrative, my brother and I thought we'd give it a try in the United States. The only difference was that we had to collect money from the customers directly instead of being paid a salary.

Each household was supposed to pay us eight dollars per month, and one dollar of that was our profit. Collecting payment was often a problem, because our English was limited and people sometimes pretended not to understand what we were saying. More often than not, we would show up for payment to discover that the customer had moved away without notice.

One day, I was bitten by a customer's dog—a big, aggressive brute that had been chasing me every morning for weeks. I had complained to the dog's owner, but he never took me seriously. After the attack I showed him the doctor's receipt and the bite marks on my leg, but the man just pushed me away and said, "Not my dog!" He never reimbursed me for my medical expenses, so I essentially delivered papers to 150 houses without pay.

The most rewarding part of newspaper delivery was the tips. The custom doesn't exist in Japan, so it was a thrill to get paid extra for good service. As in Japan, I made a point of throwing the paper as accurately as possible—even keeping my own personal-best score sheet to make the mornings more exciting. Some months, my brother and I made more in tips than we did in salary.

For the next year and a half, my family continued to face financial difficulties. We moved frequently from place to place in an attempt to find affordable rent, and although the challenges were great, we continued to persevere. We knew we were building a resilient spirit that would serve us well in the future, but at the time, we had no idea what was in store for us.

We struggled more than I could have imagined, but our faith remained strong. We knew that God would handle anything that we could not, because He has a way of building your character in difficult times. I believe that our hardships were His way of preparing us for something bigger and better. With a heart filled with faith, anything is possible.

janglish roll

Named for the blend of Japanese and English I used
when I first arrived in the U.S.

½ sheet nori (dried seaweed)

4½ ounces sushi rice (page 41)

½ teaspoon fresh garlic, minced

3 ounces sushi-grade Canadian albacore tuna, raw

1 ume (Japanese plum or apricot), pitted and thinly sliced*

kaiware (daikon radish sprouts) to taste*

2 shiso leaves (a mint-like herb)*

8 salmon pearls (large, orange-colored salmon roe)

Prepare the roll following the instructions on page 26. Start with
a sheet of nori, and top it with sushi rice, garlic, half the tuna
(1½ ounces), sliced ume, and kaiware. Roll up. Top the roll with
shiso leaves and remaining 1½ ounces of tuna.

Using a sharp knife, cut the roll into bite-sized pieces. Transfer
to a serving plate.

Top each piece with a salmon pearl.

Available at Asian markets

mᶜcooney's tempura

Named for the way we spell Mikuni on St. Patrick's Day

2 ounces sushi-grade Japanese tai (red sea bream), raw

½ teaspoon fresh garlic, minced

1 ume (Japanese plum or apricot), pitted and thinly sliced*

4 shiso leaves (a mint-like herb)*

vegetable oil, enough for deep-frying

tempura batter (page 33)

½ teaspoon yuzu salt (recipe at right)

Wrap the tai, garlic, and sliced ume in shiso leaves and skewer with a toothpick.

Heat vegetable oil in a deep pan to 350 degrees. Lightly dip the wrap in tempura batter, then transfer to a deep fryer basket. Submerge the roll in the hot oil and fry until crisp. Remove carefully and drain on a rack. Transfer to a serving plate.

Serve with yuzu salt.

Available at Asian markets

YUZA SALT

8 parts sea salt

1 part yuzu juice*

In a small saucepan, cook salt and yuzu juice over low heat for two minutes.

CHAPTER 4

HIGH SCHOOL HORRORS

"In the school I went to, they asked a kid to prove the law of gravity and he threw the teacher out of the window."

—Rodney Dangerfield,
*American Comedian and
Actor*

Adjusting to high school can be tough for just about any American teenager. When you toss a Japanese kid with less-than-perfect English into the mix, it's a recipe for disaster.

I had a vision of what high school would be like, and to me it was a perfect world. Everyone spoke fluent English, the girls all looked like Sharon Stone, and the boys were all variations of Danny Zuko, the character played by John Travolta in *Grease*. Was I in for a surprise!

The first high school I attended—there were three in all—was Hiram Johnson in Sacramento. The student body consisted mostly of minorities, and languages like Spanish and Tagalog were more common than English. These kids helped ensure that my education was extremely well-rounded, as they taught me lessons that did not exist in any textbook—like how to use a switchblade, the best ways to cut class, effective fighting techniques, and one hundred ways to disrespect your teacher. Unlike Japanese students, who play by the rules because they fear discipline, my classmates in America were afraid of nothing.

FAKE IT TILL YOU MAKE IT

Fighting, using drugs, and drinking alcohol were common occurrences on campus, and these stark behavioral differences shocked me. I remember walking down the hallway one day to find a group of seven African-American boys picking on a little Asian kid. As I got closer, I realized that the boy was my brother. I ran over to help him, and the boys greeted me with a stereotypical question: "You're Japanese...do you know karate?" I'd never practiced any martial arts in my life, but it seemed like a good opportunity to bluff. I demonstrated some made-up moves, threw in a few sounds effects, and impressed the heck out of them. They walked away without throwing another punch.

This incident marked the beginning of an attitude that I would carry with me throughout most of high school: sometimes you have to pretend to know something even if you're completely clueless. This philosophy helped me learn to adapt to my new life at times, but some of my lessons came with an embarrassingly high price tag.

HARD KNOCKS

Most Americans can look back on their high school years and remember with fondness many of the typical defining moments: football games, parties, proms, and social groups. Sadly, my memories are marked mostly by humiliating and awkward experiences. One event in particular makes me cringe to this day.

A very pretty girl, half Caucasian and half Japanese, invited me to the school's homecoming dance—or so I thought. I had no idea what the affair entailed, but there was no way I was going to turn down such an attractive young lady. I said yes and nodded happily, then asked my friends to fill me in on dance protocol.

They informed me that I needed to buy tickets, get her flowers, pick her up at her house, and arrange transportation to the dance. Great, except for a couple of minor details: I had no car and no idea where she lived. I decided that the best thing to do would be to meet her at the school and walk into the dance together. The next time I saw her, I told her I'd see her outside the auditorium on the night of the event, and she agreed.

On the big night, I walked to the school—a feeling of excitement and anticipation building in my chest. *I have a date with one of the most beautiful girls at Hiram Johnson!* I saw her standing in front of the auditorium, a good-looking Caucasian boy at her side. *What's he doing here? Is he her date? But wait—I thought I was her date.* Confused and panicky, I approached them, clutching her corsage and the dance tickets in my shaking hands.

"Didn't you invite me to the dance?" I asked her.

She smiled sweetly and replied, "What I said was, 'Why don't you invite someone to the dance?'"

Lost in translation, I guess.

I tried to make the best of a terrible situation by going to the dance anyway. As the night wore on, my friends made a circle around me while I danced in the middle by myself. The few friends I had were very good to me, and I was grateful for each and every one of them. They taught me a little about their culture and a lot about surviving it.

LIVING AND LEARNING

As I continued on through high school, I underwent many different experiences—some more memorable than others, some harder to swallow. I can still recall walking into class one morning in December. As I crossed the front of the room heading toward my seat, some of the kids starting shooting rubber bands at me. Over and over again, I was stung for no apparent reason. All of a sudden, they yelled out in unison, "Happy Pearl Harbor Day!"

I had no idea what they meant, so I made my way to my seat, smiling with my hands in the air. It wasn't until much later in life that I found out I was the butt of a cruel ethnic joke. I have always tried to give people the benefit of the doubt, but sometimes it worked against me. All I could do was learn from my naïveté and move forward.

In my senior year, I transferred to Oakmont High in Roseville, California, which was the nicest, safest high school that I attended. It was still difficult for me to fit in because my spare time was spent working instead of participating in sports and social activities, but I felt more accepted there than I had anywhere else.

That same year, 1987, my family finally got serious about opening our very own restaurant. With no credit, no connections, and no business experience—in fact, with nothing more than our trust in God—we decided to embark on our dream of bringing authentic Japanese cuisine to a very American society.

sureak roll

Named for what I am: a sushi freak

½ sheet nori (dried seaweed)

4½ ounces sushi rice (page 41)

1 ounce sushi-grade kyushi hamachi (yellowtail), raw

2 whole asparagus spears, blanched

sansho pepper to taste*

1½ ounces sushi-grade Tasmanian ocean trout, raw

kaiware (daikon radish sprouts) to taste*

1 rakkyo (pickled onion bulb), thinly sliced*

1 teaspoon lemon zest

1 teaspoon tenkasu (tempura crumbs)*

Sureak Sauce (recipe at right)

Prepare the roll following the instructions on page 26. Start with a sheet of nori, and top it with sushi rice, kyushi hamachi, and asparagus spears. Sprinkle with sansho pepper. Roll up. Top the roll with trout.

Using a sharp knife, cut the roll into bite-sized pieces. Transfer to a serving plate.

Garnish each piece with kaiware, rakkyo, lemon zest, and tenkasu. Serve topped with Sureak Sauce.

SUREAK SAUCE

1 tablespoon yuzu juice*

½ tablespoon lemon juice

3 tablespoons soy sauce

¼ teaspoon fresh garlic, minced

pinch of black pepper

In a small bowl, whisk all ingredients until well blended.

*Available at Asian markets

CHAPTER **5**

THE MIRACLE THAT
MADE MIKUNI

 "I believe that each of
us has a calling that is
as individual as a face,
and success comes
from finding what you
love and sharing it
with others by letting
God lead the way."

—*Taro Arai, Master Sushi
Chef and Author*

W
hen you find your passion, you also find your purpose. Doing something that you enjoy fulfills both your life and your soul, which is an undeniable gift. I've heard people say that if you enjoy what you do, you'll never work a day in your life. I believe that to be true.

Each day I wake up and feel so blessed that I am able to do something that I absolutely love. It hasn't always been easy, but the early struggles have helped me appreciate today's bounty even more.

AN UNEXPECTED BLESSING

Once we made the decision to open our own restaurant, my father turned to his faith for guidance. Everyone in the family was well aware that we had limited resources to pursue this dream of ours. In fact, our credentials consisted solely of my mother's extraordinary cooking abilities and my father's passion. But with no money and no concept of a business plan, how could we possibly turn our vision into a reality?

At the time, we were all working in my aunt's Japanese restaurant, where my mother did the cooking and my father waited on tables. One evening, a distinguished Japanese gentleman came in for dinner and ordered the tempura.

"This is exactly like my hometown food," he said, looking very pleased and a bit nostalgic.

He and my father engaged in conversation, and they discovered that they grew up in the same town of Kyushu. The man said he was a doctor in Japan and was currently visiting Roseville, where he owned several houses. He gave my father one of his business cards and told him to call if he wanted to discuss the possibility of renting one of the homes.

My dad telephoned the man the following day. During their conversation, he talked about his vision of opening a restaurant. Unexpectedly, the man asked my dad for his bank account number. Because my dad was always a trusting soul—and because his bank account was consistently close to empty—he gave the man the information.

The next morning, when my dad's curiosity prompted him to check his account balance, he discovered that it contained an additional three hundred thousand dollars!

Because our new friend was touched by my family's dream—and because he had been carried back to his childhood by my mother's cooking—he believed that our restaurant could be a success, and he wanted to lend us the money to make it happen. There was no paperwork or promissory note. No verbal promise. Just a generous man's faith in my father's ambitions—a blessing to us all.

LOCATION, LOCATION, LOCATION

Thanks to our benefactor, we were suddenly in a position to start searching for space for our new restaurant. We ended up in Fair Oaks, which, at the time, was essentially in the middle of nowhere. Thirty minutes outside of Sacramento, it was a predominantly residential area without much commercial property. Could we actually lure the residents out of their homes to dine on strange ethnic cuisine?

Once again, faith took over. Convinced that God would look out for us, my father continued to move forward. As construction on the project began, his belief in its potential grew stronger and stronger.

One day, he announced to the family that he would call the restaurant Mikuni, which means "kingdom of God." After all, it was God's mercy that had brought a kind and benevolent stranger into our lives, allowing my father's passion to blossom and grow.

My Mother, The Chef

Oishii means "delicious" in Japanese, and that's precisely how I describe my mom's cooking. Her love and passion shine through with a devotion you can almost taste, and to me, she is the best chef in the world. I used to love watching her cook when I was a child, and I credit her with opening my eyes to the culinary world. With no formal schooling or training, she was responsible for helping to create our American dream.

let's roll

Named for my family's decision to finally start our own restaurant

½ sheet nori (dried seaweed)

4½ ounces sushi rice (page 41)

2 tempura shrimp (Use tempura batter recipe on page 33. Dip shrimp in batter and deep fry until golden.)

¼ avocado, sliced

Magic Sauce (recipe at right)

Oishii Applesauce (recipe at right)

1 green onion, thinly sliced

¼ teaspoon masago (smelt roe)*

Prepare the roll following the instructions on page 26. Start with a sheet of nori, and top it with sushi rice and tempura shrimp. Roll up. Top the roll with sliced avocado.

Using a sharp knife, cut the roll into bite-sized pieces. Transfer to a serving plate.

Spread Magic Sauce on one side of a plate and Oishii Apple Sauce on the other. Lay the sliced roll on top, and garnish each piece with sliced green onion and masago.

MAGIC SAUCE

1½ teaspoons mirin (sweet Japanese cooking wine)*
1 pasteurized egg yolk
¼ teaspoon sea salt
white pepper to taste
1 teaspoon rice vinegar
½ cup vegetable oil
½ teaspoon soy sauce
½ teaspoon momiji oroshi (recipe at right)
½ tablespoon sriracha sauce (hot sauce)*

In a small saucepan, bring the mirin to a boil over high heat, reduce heat to medium, and continue to cook on a low boil until the alcohol burns off, about 5 minutes. Set aside to cool.

In a small bowl, whisk the egg yolk with sea salt, white pepper, and rice vinegar. Mix in the vegetable oil a little at a time.

When the mirin has cooled, add it to the egg yolk mixture. Stir in soy sauce, momiji oroshi, and sriracha sauce. Whisk until well blended.

OISHII APPLESAUCE

1 tablespoon dashi (recipe at right)
2 tablespoons soy sauce
3 tablespoons sake
3 tablespoons mirin (sweet Japanese cooking wine)*
1 tablespoon sugar
5 tablespoons organic applesauce
1 teaspoon cornstarch
1 teaspoon water

In a small saucepan, mix prepared dashi, soy sauce, sake, mirin, sugar, and applesauce. Cook over low heat until sugar is dissolved, about 4 minutes.

Mix cornstarch with water until well blended. Add it to the saucepan a little at a time until the mixture is slightly thickened, about 1 minute.

Available at Asian markets

Momiji Oroshi

3-ounce piece daikon, cut into small pieces

2 tablespoons water

¼ teaspoon cayenne pepper

1 teaspoon paprika

In a blender, purée daikon with water. Strain the mixture and let drain for 5 minutes. Transfer to a small bowl, and whisk in cayenne and paprika.

Dashi (Japanese Soup Stock)

2 (4-inch-square) pieces kombu (dried kelp)*
½ ounce katsuo bushi (bonito flakes), about 2 cups*
2½ quarts water

Place kombu and katsuo bushi in a 4-quart saucepan, cover with water, and soak for 1 hour.

Set the saucepan over medium heat and bring almost to boiling. Remove kombu and katsuo bushi. Increase the heat to high and bring remaining liquid to a boil. Strain the liquid through a fine mesh strainer or several layers of cheesecloth.

Can be refrigerated in an airtight container up to 1 week, or frozen up to 1 month.

CHAPTER **6**

THE GRAND OPENING

 "More than that, we
rejoice in our sufferings,
knowing that suffering
produces endurance,
and endurance
produces character,
and character
produces hope, and
hope does not put us to
shame, because God's
love has been poured
into our hearts through
the Holy Spirit who has
been given to us."

—Romans 5:3-5

As Mikuni began to take shape, we found ourselves repeating one Japanese word over and over again: *shippai*. It doesn't mean accomplishment...or fulfillment...or dream come true. It doesn't mean happiness...or attainment...or even gratitude. *Shippai* means mistake, and we made plenty of those in our first months of doing business.

One might think that three hundred thousand dollars would easily cover the costs of opening a restaurant back in the eighties, but with limited English and no connections within the community, making a deal was a lot more difficult. Because we had no idea what things were supposed to cost, we ended up paying contractors huge sums of money for basic jobs: fifteen thousand dollars for lighting that should have been two thousand dollars, a ten-thousand-dollar stove hood for fifty thousand dollars. We were naïve and believed everything people told us, and this lack of business savvy and absence of a business plan led to an inevitable result: we quickly progressed from operating blindly to falling off track to being in way over our heads.

PUTTING IT ALL TOGETHER

Our total restaurant space was thirty-five hundred square feet. Although that's standard for a decent-sized dining area, my mother requested that a third of the space be devoted to the kitchen. She wanted eight burners, three deep fryers, a huge grill, and two large woks. Once we accommodated her wishes and created the perfect kitchen, I looked at the area that was left and couldn't help but wonder where the patrons would sit.

My dad had done most of the purchasing for Mikuni, from the kimonos in the window to the antique dining-room furnishings. The tables were different shapes and sizes—creating an interesting look, but taking up more room than necessary. The chairs were bulky and heavy—giving the appearance of sturdiness, but revealing an inherent wobbliness whenever anyone sat down. It was a hodgepodge of a dining room, but its welcoming atmosphere was undeniable.

Each family member was assigned a different job. My sister worked as the hostess, greeting guests with her friendly smile and charming personality. My dad often assisted her, bowing in welcome and thanking guests as they left. My mother did most of the cooking, and because my brother and I usually helped her in the kitchen, none of the customers even knew me until we added the sushi bar. All of us maintained a fast and frenzied pace, and if we had known how much work it would take to run a restaurant, we might have abandoned the idea. But our doors were open, and there was no turning back.

THE EARLY DAYS

My dad decided that all food and drinks would be complimentary for the first three days, thinking it was a good way to introduce diners to Mikuni's Japanese fare. The response was overwhelming, with dozens of people arriving for lunch and dinner to take advantage of the free food. The huge turnout was very encouraging, and we anticipated equally busy days following our trial run.

When day four rolled around—our first opportunity to make money—my family was buzzing with excitement. But instead of racing around and serving customers, we spent the entire day and night just staring at each other. Not a single diner showed up.

Eventually, as the weeks went by, customers began to trickle in. I hired my friend Scott to play the piano during dinner hours, and the music was a nice touch. Since everyone in my family—with the exception of my dad—plays piano, we took turns to add some variety. The diners seemed to enjoy it, and it enhanced the already warm and pleasant atmosphere that we tried so hard to establish.

In the beginning, it was hard to gauge how many customers we should prepare for. Twenty? Forty? Six? Fearful that we might run out of food and ruin our reputation before it was even established, we often made more than we needed just to be safe.

All of our recipes were very time-consuming, since each item was made from scratch. From potstickers and sushi rolls to teriyaki and sukiyaki, meals were lovingly created by my mother's skilled hands. We also featured several traditional dishes that took a long time to prepare, but people rarely ordered them because they had no idea what things like *oden* and *champon* were. I avidly read cookbooks to learn as much as I could to try to help my mother, but since I was still in high school and had to focus on my studies, there never seemed to be enough hours in the day to do everything that needed to be done.

WHAT WERE WE THINKING?

Our days were long—very long. I was up each morning at seven o'clock to be in school by eight. I was able to leave at noon, because I had taken a few college classes that freed me from some of the high-school requirements. I would show up at the restaurant just in time for lunch, work until three, and then begin preparing for dinner. We remained open until ten at night, spent a couple of hours cleaning up, and ate dinner as a family with our staff at midnight. This was the routine, six days a week.

Mikuni was closed on Sundays so we could attend church services, but this didn't relieve us from the responsibility of cooking. Instead, my mom established the One Dollar Lunch and provided food for all of our church members—some days as many as 100 people. We used to do the same thing when we lived in Japan, which is how my mother learned to cook for large numbers of people.

In addition, my father offered free dinner to everyone who attended his sermon on the first Sunday of every month. Given my parents' generosity to the church community, I worked seven days a week without a day off for the first five years. I honestly couldn't complain because my parents were working longer hours than I was, but the harder we worked, the more we struggled.

After one year of operation, my family felt overburdened and discouraged. We decided to cut our losses and sell the restaurant before we were forced to file bankruptcy. We put Mikuni on the market for one hundred fifty thousand dollars—half the amount we used to create it.

I can still remember the Chinese man who came by to look at the place with the intention of buying it. He walked in, took a quick look around, chuckled to himself, and walked out shaking his head. What was he thinking? What were *we* thinking when we took on this project?

A TEST OF FAITH

We began to question every choice we had made up to that point. *Why did we move to America? Why did we think that opening a restaurant would earn us a stable living? Why did we dream so big?*

When situations become challenging, you either dig a little deeper or walk away defeated. After briefly considering giving up, we opted to dig. My father always said that we must stay strong when we feel as if we're being conquered, because it is that strength and faith that define us. I reminded myself of the Mikuni logo, which features a cross and bears two Ps to represent the words *purpose* and *praise*. I had to believe that if I did everything I could, God would do what I could not.

SUSHIFYING SACRAMENTO

Opening a Japanese restaurant was not popular with my high school friends. I often thought we should have opted for the kind of place they could relate to—like a McDonald's (or, as I pronounced it back then: Makudonarudo).

I begged my classmates to visit Mikuni and try our food, but the response was always the same: "Raw fish? Gross!" Although their negative reactions made me sad and a bit offended, I understood that sushi was a totally foreign concept to most Americans. It would take several years, but that would change.

In 2007, Oakmont High School invited me to be a special guest speaker. I was excited to go back to my old campus, but I wasn't sure what to expect. When I walked in, more than fifty kids wearing Mikuni T-shirts greeted me. My eyes filled with tears—oh, how the times had changed! I had always wanted to be the cool kid in high school, and although I was no longer a kid, I had definitely nailed the "cool" part.

Photo at right:
Taro Arai and Mitsuna Nishioka serving happy guests at the sushi bar

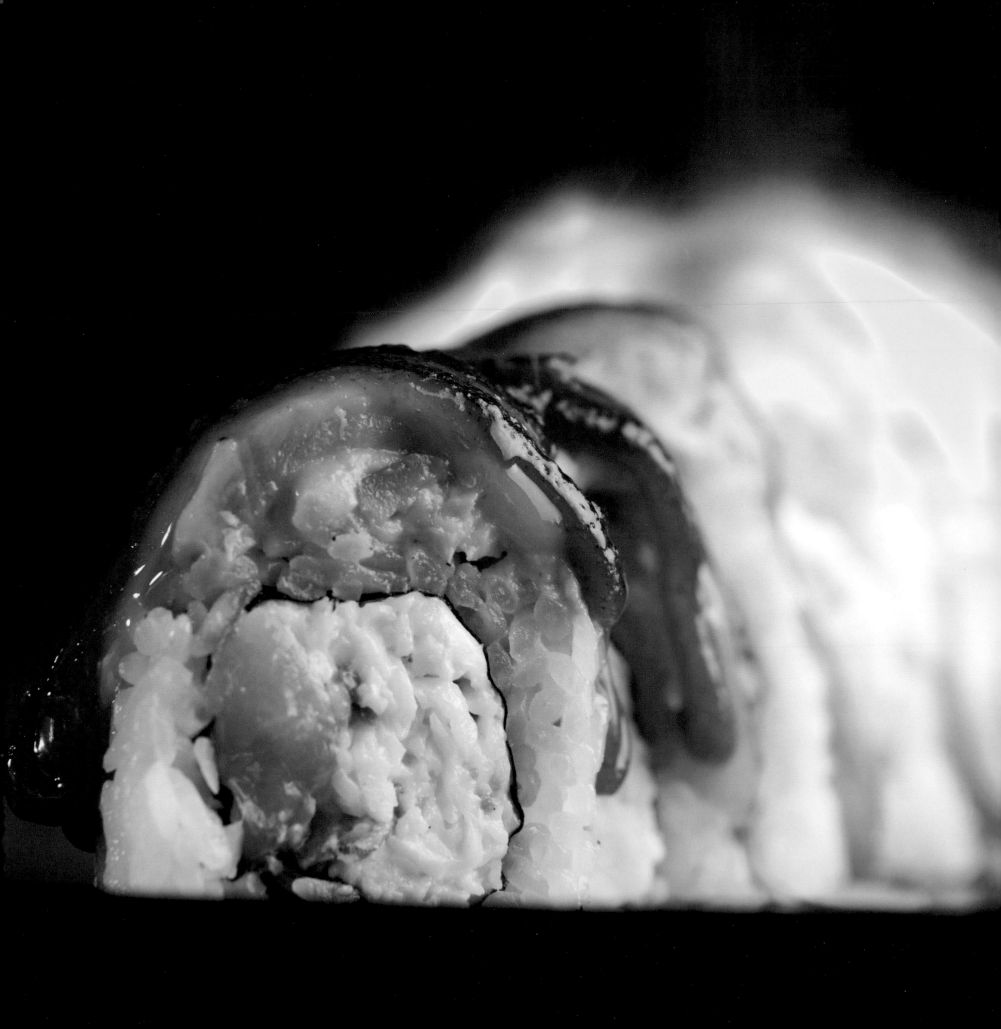

genesis roll

Named for our restaurant's new beginning:
"And God said 'Let there be light'; and there was light." (Genesis 1:3)

½ sheet nori (dried seaweed)

4½ ounces sushi rice (page 41)

1 fresh Boston scallop, sliced

3 fresh shrimp, boiled

½ ounce cream cheese

1 ounce Snow Crab Mix (recipe at right)

¼ avocado, sliced

1½ ounces fresh Alaskan king salmon, boiled

1 tablespoon American Dream Sauce (page 33)

1 tablespoon Purpose and Praise Sauce (recipe at right)

½ tablespoon Oishii Applesauce (page 61)

Prepare the roll following the instructions on page 26. Start with a sheet of nori, and top it with sushi rice, sliced scallop, shrimp, cream cheese, and Snow Crab Mix. Roll up. Top the roll with sliced avocado and king salmon.

Using a sharp knife, cut the roll into bite-sized pieces. Transfer to a serving plate.

Drizzle American Dream Sauce and Purpose and Praise Sauce over the top of the sliced roll. Using a food torch, carefully caramelize the sauces until they are lightly browned. Top each piece of the roll with a tiny dollop of Oishii Applesauce.

SNOW CRAB MIX

1 ounce snow crab, boiled
1 teaspoon Magic Sauce (page 61)

In a small bowl, mix crab and Magic Sauce until well blended.

PURPOSE AND PRAISE SAUCE

½ teaspoon mirin (sweet Japanese cooking wine)*
1 pasteurized egg yolk
¼ teaspoon sea salt
white pepper to taste
1 teaspoon rice vinegar
½ cup vegetable oil
1 teaspoon soy sauce
¾ tablespoon sugar
shichimi togarashi (Japanese spice blend) to taste*
¼ teaspoon garlic powder
¾ tablespoon white miso*
¼ teaspoon powdered taco seasoning

In a small saucepan, bring the mirin to a boil over high heat, reduce heat to medium, and continue to cook on a low boil until the alcohol burns off, about 5 minutes. Set aside to cool.

In a small bowl, whisk the egg yolk with sea salt, white pepper, and rice vinegar. Mix in the vegetable oil a little at a time.

When the mirin has cooled, add it to the egg yolk mixture. Stir in soy sauce, sugar, shichimi togarashi, garlic powder, miso, and taco seasoning. Whisk until well blended.

Available at Asian markets

CHAPTER **7**

GROWING PAINS

 "Anything that can

go wrong, will go

wrong."

— Murphy's Law

When I arrived in America, I didn't know about this thing called Murphy's Law. I'd always had a highly optimistic attitude, and I believed that things would inevitably turn out for the best. My favorite sayings were "No problem!" and "Better than nothing!"—phrases I used over and over again each time I was faced with an obstacle. During the first five years of trying to establish Mikuni, I would utter those words about a million times.

One Sunday morning, I drove to church with about three thousand dollars cash in the car—the proceeds from a full weekend of restaurant sales. I didn't think the money would be safe in my house, so it seemed best to keep it close to me. I parked in front of the church, and in my haste to open the door to let a few of the worshippers inside, I forgot to lock my car. When I realized what I had done, I raced back to discover that the door on the passenger side was wide open and the money was gone. One of the church members told me she had seen a man on a bicycle riding away from my car, and even though I called the police, the thief was never found.

Well, I thought, *I still have my God and my family, so I am wealthy beyond measure. I still have my health, so I can work to make money again. I still have this life, so I can enjoy the journey. No problem!*

On another occasion, I gave my truck key to the Mikuni dishwasher so he could drive to the grocery store to pick up some vegetables. He never returned with the vegetables or the truck, because he traded it for drugs. By the time the police found it, it had no engine, no tires, and no seats.

Well, I thought, *I still have a place to work, so I am more fortunate than many. I have car insurance, so the replacement cost is covered. I still have my faith, even though people have taken advantage of me. Better than nothing!*

MURPHY'S LAW WINS OUT

In spite of my unyielding optimism, my family struggled more than we ever could have imagined during Mikuni's early years. The more hours we worked, the more debt we incurred. The more energy we put into solving problems, the more challenges we faced. Like a band of weary wanderers mired in quicksand, the harder we labored to get free, the deeper we sank. Even though negative issues sometimes turned out okay, the emotional price we paid to get to the other side was often incredibly high.

One night, a restaurant patron asked if she could buy one of the kimonos in the display window. My dad had brought it from Japan, and it was very beautiful and very expensive. We quoted her a price of two thousand dollars, and she wrote us a check on the spot. We were thrilled, because business was slow and we needed all the income we could get.

Unfortunately, her check bounced. We had no idea who she was, where she lived, or what to do. All we had was the returned check bearing her illegible scribbles. Time to call the police again.

In a few days, they discovered that she lived in the apartment building right behind Mikuni, so they managed to get the kimono back for us. Shortly afterward, I saw her walking past the restaurant, smiling broadly and waving at me as if nothing had happened. *No problem!*

Our first bartender at Mikuni was a former football player who stood over six feet tall and weighed more than 200 pounds. He was good at his job and was usually very kind to me, but he could be moody and surly to others.

One day, he spoke in a very derogatory way to a female member of the kitchen staff. When she walked up to confront him, he punched her in the face—so hard that she fell flat on the floor. She began cursing at him, then called her husband—all six-foot-two, three hundred pounds of him—to come to the restaurant to fight the bartender. He was there in a flash, and soon fists were flying all over the place as the two hulks went at it. We were frantic because we didn't know what to do, so we relied on the usual solution when trouble reared its head.

Hello, police? It's your good friend Taro.

We had no choice but to fire the bartender, assuming that letting him go would eliminate any more conflicts. But much to our shock and dismay, he filed a lawsuit against us, stating that we did nothing to stop the fight and that we owed him a year's salary as compensation. We didn't know anything about going to court, so we hired a lawyer and turned to God for help. Our prayers were answered almost immediately, because the bartender never showed up and the case was dropped.

In 1991, when I was twenty-one, my dad decided to add a sushi bar to the restaurant. To my surprise, he asked me to quit school—making him perhaps the first and only Asian parent to ever do that!—and become a sushi chef. I was about to transfer to UCLA, but instead I said, "No problem!"

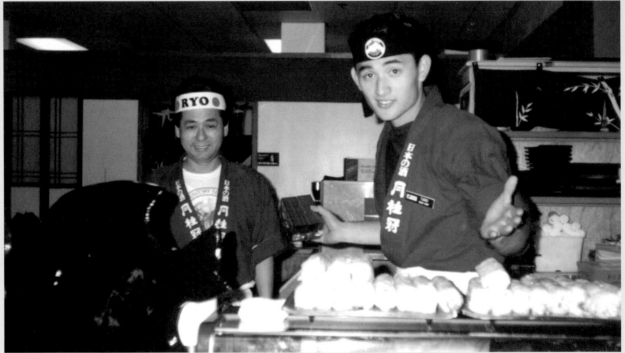

DAD MEETS MURPHY

Waiting on tables was not a very pleasant job for my father. Between serving the meals, cleaning up afterward, and settling the bills, he spent most of his days and evenings rushing around the restaurant without a break.

One afternoon, while bussing a table, he realized that the patron who'd been sitting there didn't pay. He dashed out of the restaurant and started chasing the man down the street. As luck would have it, my dad was a competitive runner throughout his youth, so he had no trouble catching up to the non-paying customer. He humbly asked for payment for the food, and the man said he had left the money under his plate. Embarrassed beyond belief, my father apologized over and over as he bowed his head and backed away. Upon returning to the restaurant, he discovered that the man had lied. There was no money to be found anywhere on the table. Feeling defeated and exhausted, my dad shouldered on through the rest of the day.

Carrying on in spite of the heaviest burdens is what defines my father, and the following story demonstrates his strong sense of commitment.

I heard his scream before I knew what had happened. I raced toward the sound, and saw my father about to jump into a large trash bin filled with ice. He had noticed that the lid on our large deep fryer had been left open after it was cleaned, and he ran over to close it. He slipped and fell, knocking over a large bucket filled with 360-degree oil that had been emptied from the fryer, and severely burned both of his legs.

When we took him to the hospital, the doctor who treated him said he would not be able to work for six weeks, but my father ignored the directive. After all, he had a restaurant to run! He continued to show up like clockwork every day, walking as if he were maneuvering his way across thin ice.

Kitchen accidents were not uncommon to my father. He was never particularly comfortable working around the equipment, and he endured more than his share of cuts and bruises. Now that he was

a restaurant owner, his graceful, smooth hands transformed into wounded, rough ones as he made the change from holding books to wielding knives.

SAYONARA TO MURPHY AT LAST!

Launching Mikuni was like wandering through shadows. The only thing we knew for certain was that we would rather walk in the dark with God than walk in the light by ourselves.

My dad kept reminding us of the importance of having a solid foundation on which to build our dream. He said we had to work harder than anyone and trust that God would do his best for us. In spite of his attempts to encourage and inspire us, I recently found out that he spent a lot of time crying and praying in those early years, resisting the temptation to return to Japan and never think about Mikuni again.

In 1991, when I was twenty-one, my dad decided to add a sushi bar to the restaurant. To my surprise, he asked me to quit school—making him perhaps the first and only Asian parent to ever do that!—and become a sushi chef. I was about to transfer to UCLA, but instead I said, "No problem!"

A few months later, armed with dozens of new sushi books purchased in San Francisco, we began construction on the sushi bar. Little did we know that we were doing it illegally, because we were clueless about the need to get a permit from the county. All we knew was that we were continuing to move forward and build that deep foundation my father always talked about.

After five years of losing money every month, having very few customers, and still not knowing quite what we were doing, we could feel that change was in the air. Instead of focusing on adversity and looking down in sorrow, we looked up for God's mercy and anticipated His blessing.

In 1992, the California Restaurant Association honored Mikuni with an award for Best Kept Secret—the first of many awards to come and the start of our new chapter.

murphy's roll

Named for Murphy's Law: everything that shouldn't be
in a sushi roll is in this one!

1 sheet wheat paper*

½ ounce barbecued eel*

1 ounce fresh mango, thinly sliced

¼ avocado, sliced

Apricot Sauce (recipe at right)

edible flower

vegetable oil, enough for deep-frying

tempura batter (page 33)

pinch Nerds candy**

Prepare the roll following the instructions on page 26. Start
with a sheet of wheat paper, and top with barbecued eel, sliced
mango, and avocado. Roll up.

Heat vegetable oil in a deep pan to 350 degrees. Transfer the
roll to a deep-fryer basket. Submerge the roll in the hot oil and
fry until crisp. Remove carefully and drain on a rack. When cool
enough to handle, slice into bite-sized pieces and transfer to a
serving plate.

Lightly dip the edible flower in tempura batter, then transfer to
a deep-fryer basket. Submerge the flower in the hot oil used for
the roll, and fry until crisp. Remove carefully and drain on a rack
until cool enough to handle.

Spoon Apricot Sauce over the roll. Garnish with tempura-fried
flower and Nerds candy.

Available at Asian markets
**Sold by Nestlé under their Willy Wonka Candy Company brand*

APRICOT SAUCE

¼ cup apricot jam
½ teaspoon brown mustard
⅛ teaspoon prepared
wasabi

Combine all ingredients and
mix well.

CHAPTER **8**

MY FATHER'S VISION

 "May the God of
hope fill you with
all joy and peace in
believing, so that
by the power of the
Holy Spirit you may
abound in hope."

—Romans 15:13

"I have a vision."

It was 1992, and my dad made the announcement as we were cleaning up after a long day at the restaurant. His voice was as calm, casual, and confident as if he'd said, "The sun is going to shine tomorrow."

I looked at him curiously, waiting for him to go on.

"God has shown me that we will soon have one thousand customers a day."

My dad is like Moses—a man of unshakable faith with an unobstructed connection to his Maker. I wanted to believe in him the way he believes in God, but it wasn't always easy.

Although our sales had doubled since we first opened Mikuni, we were averaging just under seven hundred dollars—or about fifty diners—per day. How on earth could we boost that by 2000 percent? Although such a dramatic increase seemed to defy logic, one thing was certain: whenever my dad prayed, something wonderful happened.

LEARNING MY WAY AROUND THE SUSHI BAR

Since my father knew nothing about sushi, he turned over responsibility for running our new sushi bar to me. The idea of complete freedom was appealing, but I didn't have a clue what I was doing. We eventually hired my brother's friend Masa to work with me, which was a mixed blessing. Masa had recently arrived from Japan, and although he was a skilled sushi chef and a very friendly and agreeable guy, his English was almost nonexistent.

One day, a regular guest sat down at the sushi bar and said, "Masa, you're the best! Please make me anything you would like—except saba [mackerel]."

Masa smiled his customary smile and went straight to work, sushi knife flying and nimble fingers rolling. After several minutes, I heard the customer shriek, "Taro, please help me. I can't eat this!"

"Saba" was the only word that Masa understood when the man spoke, so he made saba roll, saba sashimi, and saba everything else. I immediately explained the problem to him, and he happily prepared a selection of non-mackerel food.

Maybe if I couldn't make it as a sushi chef, I might be able to get a job as an interpreter.

Masa was a big part of Mikuni from the very beginning, and many customers grew to know and love him. Today, he remains a vital part of our operation, delivering sushi rice from our central kitchen to all the restaurants.

DOOMED TO FAILURE?

In the midst of our struggles to establish a name and reputation for Mikuni, a book was published about how to have a successful Japanese restaurant in America. The good news: Mikuni was mentioned. The bad news: the writer said we were surviving only because we had no competition, and we would never be able to keep our doors open in the future.

At the time, Sacramento was home to about one hundred Japanese restaurants. Was it true that we were still in business only because those numbers were small? Would the appearance of more sushi places wipe us out?

For the time being, it was senseless to worry about such things. Our focus had to remain on running Mikuni, which was an all-consuming project.

Since our business was still relatively small, the fish company we used in San Francisco refused to deliver our meager orders to Sacramento. I had no choice but to drive to the Bay Area twice a week in my ancient Toyota Corona, which had 240,000 miles on it. I would leave my house at one thirty in the morning and arrive at the fish company at about four thirty, because I had to stop at least once an hour to let the engine cool down. I would then drive back to Sacramento, deliver the fish to the restaurant, and head to school (and the occasional desk nap). As soon as my morning classes were over, I would return to Mikuni and go to work at the sushi bar.

By then Masa and I had been joined by my cousin Mitsuna, who was in high school at the time. We did everything ourselves—from peeling shrimp and boning fish to cleaning the restaurant and purchasing the food. The pressure and stress were enormous, and I tried to cope in all the wrong ways: power-eating spicy foods, drinking too much coffee, and treating sleep as if it were a luxury instead of a necessity. I ended up developing an ulcer and adding frequent hospital visits to my already harried schedule. Would the craziness never end?

Masato Matsumura (Masa) with Taro Arai

IT'S NOT WHAT YOU KNOW, BUT WHO YOU KNOW

Because I had no experience running a business, I frequently lost confidence in my ability to do so. Fortunately, I was surrounded by patrons who loyally supported Mikuni and shared my family's belief in the dream.

One day, a customer who was a big sports fan suggested that we install a television by the sushi bar so diners could watch American football. This was a completely foreign concept to me, since I grew up watching sumo wrestling and baseball in Japan. But I trusted his advice, so against my family's wishes, I brought in a 12-inch set from home.

During one Monday night game, the man asked me who I thought would win. *Why is he asking me? I know nothing about football!* But I decided to play along, so I picked the team whose uniform colors I liked best. And they won.

The following Monday, the man brought more of his friends to the restaurant, and again I was asked to pick the winner of the game. This went on for twelve weeks—"Red team." "Green team."—and by some miracle or wild stroke of luck, I was right every time. In addition to learning about football, I had the pleasure of seeing the sushi bar filled to capacity during every Monday night football game.

Besides encouraging me through some of my darkest times, these people—these new and lasting friends—helped our business grow and prosper. Without them, I fear I would not have had the faith to continue to move forward. For the rest of my life, I will be grateful to them for all they have done.

THE POWER OF LOVE

In 1993, a dream came true for me: I married the beautiful Machiko, who had been my Japanese pen pal for many years. We met when we were eleven years old, and we had our first date at fifteen. She began working for Mikuni shortly after arriving in the United States, and her presence changed everything.

Within days, people started lining up for lunch and dinner, and we grew from fifty customers a day to two hundred. The following year, we took over the yogurt shop next door and expanded—again without the necessary permits. We did all the construction work ourselves, removing all the display windows to make more room for additional tables.

By 1996, our restaurant had 120 seats and served four hundred guests per day on the weekends. We eventually enlarged our space once more—taking over a hair salon and a video store and managing to get a donut shop moved to another building—and boosted this number to five hundred. It had taken four years and we still had a long way to go, but we were halfway to reaching my dad's vision of one thousand diners.

THE MIKUNI SUSHI BUS

Mikuni is proud to be the originator of the first and only sushi bus in the world. Equipped with sofas to seat twelve and enhanced by two flat-screen televisions, the bus features an on-board chef who prepares an assortment of fresh sushi. Conveniences include hot and cold running water, an oven, and a refrigerator.

Guests can travel to the location of their choice, and our destinations have been diverse. We've gone to sporting events for tailgate parties, to wine country, to local neighborhoods for a Christmas-lights cruise, and once motored all the way to San Diego for a block party.

Can the Mikuni sushi boat or sushi jet be far behind?

miso happy scallops

Named for the fact that I'm always a joyful person

1 teaspoon sake

pinch sea salt

pinch freshly ground black pepper

2 Hokkaido scallops or large sea scallops

1 teaspoon olive oil

1.6 ounces sushi rice (page 41)

2 tablespoons Purpose and Praise Sauce (page 69)

⅛ jalapeño pepper, thinly sliced

1 chive, chopped

2 snow crab legs, boiled

½ teaspoon black tobiko caviar

pinch tenkasu (tempura crumbs)*

Koki Arai, #1 son

In a small bowl, blend the sake, sea salt, and black pepper. Add scallops, toss gently to coat, and soak for 5 minutes.

Heat a medium-sized skillet over high heat, add olive oil, and heat just until smoking. Add the scallops and cook for 10 seconds on each side. Remove scallops from pan and slice in half horizontally.

Form sushi rice into 4 balls of equal size. Place one-half sliced scallop on each rice ball. Transfer to a serving plate.

Drizzle Purpose and Praise Sauce over each rice ball. Garnish with sliced jalapeño and chopped chives.

Place crab legs on top of rice balls and garnish all with tobiko caviar and tenkasu.

*Available at Asian markets

CHAPTER **9**

UNSTOPPABLE

 "Trust in the Lord with all your heart, and do not rely on your own insight. In all your ways acknowledge Him, and He will make straight your paths."

—*Proverbs 3:5-6*

"Bakayaro!" Loosely translated, this means "idiot."

The word was screamed in my face by an elderly Japanese sushi chef who was watching me prepare *ikizukuri* (a type of sashimi made with live fish) of *tai* (red sea bream). It was a special dish that I was making for a regular customer's birthday, and since he was an avid smoker, I placed a cigarette in the mouth of the fish as a candle. The old samurai was so upset he was ready to make sashimi out of me.

He explained, as calmly as he could in his agitated state, that sushi chefs must respect fish, since without fish, we have no job...without a job, we have no income...and without income, we have no life.

Even though I was proud of my creative presentation—and continue to do things like that to this day—I had to admit that he was right. The more I learned about the traditions of making sushi, the more I realized how serious the rules were. No mayonnaise...no spicy sauces...no deep-fried foods. The list went on and on. While I have always respected the Japanese culture and its customs, I have a hard time playing by the book. After all, I came to America so I could experience freedom and the wonderful sense of discovery that goes with it.

In an attempt to comply, I kept telling myself not to take any liberties with food, but in the battle of tradition vs. experimentation, my playful nature won. I also had to be true to my belief that the most fundamental rule when preparing sushi is to give the customers what they want, no matter how bizarre it might be.

BREAKING THE RULES—AND LOVING IT

One day, a family with a young boy came into the restaurant and sat down at the sushi bar. The child immediately announced that he hated fish and didn't eat any vegetables except French fries. He then asked me to make him a SpongeBob Roll, at which point he crossed his arms over his chest and grinned, knowing he had tossed a major challenge my way.

Fortunately, I know all about SpongeBob SquarePants, so I set out to create something on the spot. I formed a square shape filled with peanut butter, French fries, and crispy rice, then topped it with thin slices of banana to make it yellow. I torched it with brown sugar and used chocolate chips for the eyes, a banana stem for the nose, and a slice of peach for the mouth. The little boy's eyes grew wider by the minute as he watched me with great intensity. I handed him the finished project with a flourish, and before he even took a bite, he shouted, "I love sushi!"

As time went by, I managed to break every rule at the sushi bar. I turned rolls inside out by placing the rice on the outside. I used avocado, which is not a classically acceptable sushi ingredient. I made sauces with the forbidden mayonnaise, turned up the heat with fiery spices, and garnished with *tobiko* (flying fish roe). My customers were pleased, but the conventional Japanese chefs who sampled my fare often accused me of being disrespectful to the sushi world.

ON A ROLL

In my opinion, sushi is a blend of traditional culture and contemporary style. The combination, when done right, can generate original, innovative dishes that get people excited. This enthusiasm, in turn, spreads globally and creates a demand for the new trend.

Fueled by these beliefs, I decided to let go and be as creative as possible—no matter how bizarre or unconventional the results might be. I quickly discovered that there is no greater compliment than the satisfied look on the face of a customer who has been delighted by something new and different.

By the late 1990s, I had created more than three hundred original Mikuni rolls. Some of them are exotic, like the Godzilla Roll, which features ten ingredients and is served with a fork and knife. Some are mysterious, like the Wonder Roll (I wonder what's in it?). Still others are downright outrageous, like the 99-cent Air Roll that is nothing more than rice wrapped in seaweed, or the $10,000 Roll that comes with a two-carat diamond. (We've actually sold a few of these.) Many are named after loyal guests, and they remain on the Mikuni menu to this day.

Another original Mikuni offering is the Birthday Wheel. Diners get to spin it on their birthday for the chance to win a prize: a bag of

Japanese rice, a restaurant gift card, or any of several gifts that range from fun to fabulous. The idea was to make Mikuni both a dining destination and a fun experience.

NEW DOORS OF OPPORTUNITY

Shortly before the turn of the century, the lines at Mikuni were growing longer every day. On weekends, it was not unusual for the wait time to be an hour and a half. By then we had fifteen sushi chefs, hired from the community at large when we finally ran out of cousins to employ. We were so busy that many of our full-time staff were working more than sixty hours a week. Was this our sign to open another restaurant?

Initially, we worried that a second location would divide our customer base and cause a poor turnout at both restaurants. We also feared that we couldn't manage to keep two places running smoothly at the same time. My dad, however, chose to trust his faith and his vision, so against the advice of many of our key workers, we opened the second Mikuni in Roseville, California, in 1999.

PARTY TIME!

To show our appreciation to our customers and to encourage new business, we threw a variety of parties over the years.

Sake Tasting Party: Guests sampled rice wine from various vendors and learned about pairing it with sushi.

Exotic Sushi Party: We served dishes that featured some of the most bizarre foods imaginable. We also held contests in wasabi making, wasabi eating, beer tasting, and even belly dancing.

Iron Chef Contest: To encourage Mikuni chefs to improve their skills, we held sushi competitions among ourselves. As time went on, I challenged other sushi chefs in the Sacramento area to join the competition...reached out to chefs in other states...and eventually brought master champions from Japan to compete with our chefs.

Mecha Ike (Just Go!): This fashion show involved local designers and hair stylists. Best of all, I got to walk down the runway with the models!

Dating Game Party: This was held primarily for the Japanese exchange students attending local colleges. It turned out to be a great way to introduce them to the community.

Sports Tournament Party: We started with a basketball tournament for employees and close friends to raise money for church. We soon added tournaments in tennis, table tennis, bowling, softball, and volleyball, but it was clear that golf tournaments would generate the most funds. In time, we raised money for both our church and other charitable organizations.

Poker Tournament Party: We raised almost ten thousand dollars during each tournament, and the money was donated to various charities.

20-80 Party: When we found out that 20 percent of our customers bring in 80 percent of our business, we held a private party for our loyal regulars.

Celebrating our 20th Anniversary

MIKUNI

1987   2007

Performance artist David Garibaldi

mr. no problem roll

Named for my reply to just about everything

1 sheet soybean wrap*

5 ounces sushi rice

1 soft shell crab

vegetable oil, enough for deep-frying

tempura batter

2 tablespoons Purpose and Praise Sauce (page 69)

½ teaspoon masago (smelt roe)*

1 green onion, thinly sliced

½ avocado, sliced

1 ounce Snow Crab Mix (page 69)

1 ounce Spicy Tuna Mix (recipe at right)

1 tablespoon Oishii Applesauce (page 61)

Prepare the roll following the instructions on page 26. Start with a soybean sheet, and top with sushi rice, leaving a ¾-inch border at the far side. Set aside.

Heat vegetable oil in a deep pan to 350 degrees. Lightly dip soft shell crab in tempura batter, then transfer to a deep-fryer basket. Submerge the crab in the hot oil and fry until crisp. Remove carefully and drain on a rack until cool enough to handle.

Chop tempura-fried crab and mix with Purpose and Praise Sauce, masago, and green onion. Spread mixture along center of roll. Roll up.

Using a sharp knife, cut the roll into bite-sized pieces. Transfer to a serving plate.

Place Snow Crab Mix and Spicy Tuna Mix on top of each piece. Spoon Oishii Applesauce over all.

Available at Asian markets

SPICY TUNA MIX

1 ounce sushi-grade yellowfin tuna, raw

½ teaspoon Spicy Freedom Sauce (page 41)

In a small bowl, mix tuna and Spicy Freedom Sauce with fork until well blended.

CHAPTER **10**

FROM CONTROLLING TO CONTENTED

 "I have learned the secret of being content in any and every situation, whether well fed or hungry, whether living in plenty or in want."

—*Philippians 4:12*

Bam! I banged my fist on the counter and threw the freshly made roll across the sushi bar. It soared over the heads of the customers and landed with a messy *plop!* on the cashier station where my sister worked. I did this time and again whenever I got mad, which was quite often once we opened our second location.

Despite the obvious progress we had made, operating two restaurants was not an easy task. Problems that we'd never even imagined cropped up on a regular basis, and I wasn't very good at dealing with them. More often than not, my temper got in the way, so there was a lot of flying fish in Mikuni Roseville.

CHANGING MY WAYS

Our sushi bar employees were from different countries, had different skill levels, and embraced different mindsets and goals. The result was barely manageable chaos.

"How long do I have to work to get my next raise?"

"Why does that chef make more money than I do?"

"When can I become a manager?"

"Can I get next Tuesday off?"

The questions flew at me with such speed and frequency that my frustration level was soaring. Most of my time was spent managing, training, and placating people, and my energy was completely depleted by closing time. I was constantly short-tempered and cranky, which certainly didn't make the adjustment period any easier.

One day, I complained bitterly to my dad about one of our employees. "He sleeps all the time! How can he accomplish anything?"

My father calmly replied, "When you both die, there will not be much of a difference between the two of you. Just remember to have a cheerful heart, since life is a journey."

He always had a way of defusing a situation and putting it in perspective, so I vowed that I would try to unwind. From that day on, whenever I felt myself getting upset, I would go behind the restaurant, slowly count to ten, do a few pull-ups on a tree branch, and pray. In

time, I was composed enough to look for a solution instead of losing my head. Eventually, a steady calmness replaced the anger, and the everyday problems became easier to handle.

DEALING WITH THE COMPETITION

Just as Mikuni Roseville was beginning to take off, several Japanese restaurants began opening in the area. We lost several sushi chefs to them, because they tended to offer more money, fewer hours, and greater management opportunities. The competition grew even worse when some of our chefs started their own restaurants and featured the dishes and sauces we taught them to make. Although we felt betrayed, we set our emotions aside and wished them well.

In 2000, we decided to build a central kitchen, where the secret of our new sauces would be safe and where we could perfect the consistency of our rice, which is the most important component of sushi. Since my parents were overworked and challenged by the speed of the day-to-day operations, they decided to work there. It was a perfect fit, because they were able to put in fewer hours and spend more time at church and leisure activities.

The central kitchen is still active today, and more than two thousand pounds of sushi rice are prepared there on a daily basis. Two employees work from ten o'clock at night to seven in the morning on that task alone. A full-time manager oversees all the supplies, ensuring that they're delivered to our six Sacramento-area restaurants every morning.

REACHING FOR THE STARS

In 2003, we opened our third location in an historic brick building in midtown Sacramento. A very skilled and talented team worked on this project, dealing with issues such as financing, build-out, and staffing. My job was to pick the color palette for the interior, and I chose pink, orange, and green. This is perhaps the most cosmopolitan of the Mikuni locations, with a vibrancy and energy that appeal to the area's fashionably hip patrons.

In the midst of all this, my parents decided to retire. I was thrilled for them, because they had worked so hard up to this point. Almost overnight, they were free to become more involved in their church, spend time with their grandchildren, and travel. My dad took up golf, and my mother went back to her beloved gardening. True contentment was theirs at last, and it had been one of my lifetime goals for them!

In 2005, we opened our fourth location—Taro's, the only restaurant that bears my name. Located at Arden Fair Mall in Sacramento, this is by far the most unusual restaurant of the bunch. Hanging silver beads separate the rooms, and the menu is equally unique. I call it free, fun-loving, and freaky, which is how I describe my own personality. The dishes extend far beyond the realm of traditional Japanese cuisine, and include pasta, lamb chops, and Kobe beef. Because I love to experiment with food, Taro's has become a testing kitchen for all the Mikuni restaurants.

A year later, Mikuni made its fifth appearance with our largest space ever—eighty-five hundred square feet, plus an outdoor patio—in Elk Grove, California. Our only freestanding building to date, it won the Gold Nugget Award for building design excellence in the Western states.

In 2007, we ventured into the Lake Tahoe region and opened a restaurant at Northstar-at-Tahoe Resort in Truckee, California. It was our sixth location...the setting is one of the most glorious on earth...and snowboarding beckoned to me. Life just couldn't get any better!

Blessed with these opportunities and successes, I finally left my temper behind for good. It was replaced by an ever-present contentment and a true appreciation for all the wonderful people who have helped shape Mikuni over the years. I learned to trust God's principles, which help us to be effective and significant leaders in a pressured and demanding world. Now, I do my best and let God do the rest.

TAKING IT TO THE NEXT LEVEL

To ensure that all Mikuni chefs are the best they can, I worked with my executive chef to create a training manual that outlines a 12-level approach to skill improvement and refinement. In order to advance to the next level, a chef must take both a written and a hands-on test.

For example, someone who is new to sushi-making starts at level 12. To progress to level 11, the aspiring chef must pass a knife safety test and be able to make ten California rolls in ten minutes. (Knife safety training is mandatory for all new employees.) By the time level 3 (management) is reached, the chef has passed the food cost test and can fillet every type of fish. With each new level comes more pay and additional benefits. This has proven to be a great way to give the chefs a series of goals and to encourage them to soar as high as they wish to go.

koki tuna flower

Named for my father and his amazing vision

5 ounces sushi-grade Canadian albacore tuna, raw

1 teaspoon lemon juice

1 teaspoon yuzu juice*

1 teaspoon sesame oil

1½ tablespoons soy sauce

1 garlic chip, crumbled

½ jalapeño pepper, thinly sliced

Cut the tuna into paper-thin slices. (For slicing instructions, see page 27.)

On a serving plate, fan out tuna slices into a flower-petal pattern. Drizzle lemon juice, yuzu juice, and sesame oil over the fish. Top with soy sauce, crumbled garlic chips, and jalapeño slices.

*Available at Asian markets

ビートルズ

ジョン

ジョージ

6-30-66

ポール

リンゴ

TOKYO

6月30日〈木〉6:30開演 // 日本武道館

40年後

タロー

1-3-06

SACTO

TARO

CHAPTER 11

UP IN THE AIR

 "Optimism is the faith that leads to achievement. Nothing can be done without hope and confidence."

—Helen Keller, American author, political activist, and lecturer

満足

"Let's open a Mikuni in Denver, Colorado!"

When one of my restaurant partners suggested this latest expansion, I was extremely skeptical. Denver is nearly nine hundred miles from Sacramento, where our reputation is firmly established. No one would know us there, so why would anyone bother to try our food? It wasn't even home to a single major Japanese restaurant chain, so could it be that the locals don't even like sushi? And isn't Denver really cold and snowy? The idea was absolutely crazy...but we did it anyway.

To be honest, I was curious to see how well we would get along outside the Sacramento region. Venturing beyond our comfort zone would be a clear indicator of our potential in other areas of the country, so it was a major test. The owner of the site offered us a very good deal and convinced us that the location was an excellent one, so we decided to take a chance.

WHAT GOES UP MUST COME DOWN

By 2008, our combined restaurant sales exceeded a mind-boggling $30 million annually and we were serving 1.5 million customers a year. To keep pace with the demand, it was necessary to order fifty tons of seafood each month. More than seven hundred people were in our employ, and we were finally able to offer reasonable hours and an attractive benefits package to our full-time employees.

At the same time, notoriety was beginning to soar. *Sacramento Magazine* had named Mikuni the Best Japanese Restaurant and the Best Sushi Restaurant in Sacramento—out of a field of three hundred dining establishments—for ten years running. The publication had also chosen me as one of the Top 100 Influential People in Sacramento, a distinction that amazed and delighted me. I had also been nominated by the California Restaurant Association as Restaurateur of the Year.

It was an incredible time, and I have to confess that all the success was going to my head. As a result, my focus started to drift. By the time we opened the doors to Mikuni in Denver—our largest and most dramatically beautiful location—I had spent more time on the golf course than I had behind the sushi bar.

Fueled by a blend of arrogance and confidence, I arrived in Denver that winter convinced of Mikuni's instant success. I turned a blind eye to the distressed economy, and I kept making lame excuses for our poor sales. "The weather is cold and the roads are icy, so people are staying home." "The weather is nice and the snow is perfect, so people are on the mountain." I simply didn't want to admit that, little by little, air was escaping from the big balloon of prosperity.

Denver wasn't the only location affected by the economic crunch. Sales in our Sacramento restaurants were down more than 10 percent, and our vendors, worried by their own dropping numbers, were giving us less payment flexibility. We tried every imaginable advertising and marketing strategy to boost business, but in the end, the only recourse was to cut staff and salaries—including my own—to stay afloat.

HOPE IN THE FACE OF HOPELESSNESS

In the midst of all these tribulations, my dad finished writing his autobiography, *My Life Is a Happy Roll*. I read it one dreary night in my Denver hotel room, my mood matching the weather. Suddenly, everything shifted. Reading my father's words, I was reminded of the importance of living with hope.

In the past, God had done so much for Mikuni, and I understood that my role was to be humble, to seek His wisdom, and to refuse to give up. I realized that serving a purpose is a lot more meaningful than achieving results...that believing in possibilities is more productive than living in fear of the unknown...that surrendering means victory, not defeat. As my father had filled me with faith and joy so many times in the past, he once again enriched my life with his wisdom.

Inspired by this renewed optimism, I worked with my partners to open the eighth Mikuni in Davis, California, in 2009. We took over an existing restaurant, so the investment costs were minimal and the time involved was just a few weeks. We seemed to be on the upswing once again.

THE SECRETS OF SUCCESS

"What college did you attend?"
"What was your major?"
"What is your talent?"

These questions were tossed at me by a reporter from one of Japan's most renowned business magazines. Curious about Mikuni's success in the United States, he wanted to know all the reasons why our business was doing so well.

I struggled with my answers, because I knew they weren't the ones the reporter expected to hear. I was clear on the fact that I had graduated from the University of Mikuni with a major in sushiology, but I couldn't say that I had any real talent. I am bad with numbers, so we have a very talented accountant/controller. I am a terrible organizer, so we have qualified people handling all the administrative work at our corporate office. I am the worst when it comes to hiring and firing people, so we have a Human Resources manager at each of our locations.

Finally, I answered. "My talent is the foresight to surround myself with people who are the very best at what they do. My gift is the ability to have fun at work every day—no matter what. I'm skilled at loving the people around me, and I'm also pretty good at delegating responsibilities to Mikuni's trusted managers. Oh, and I'm absolutely excellent at eating sushi."

While much of that never appeared in print, the fact remains that Mikuni's abundance is the result of many committed people tenaciously navigating difficult paths over the years. It is an experience that has strengthened our resolve and defined our character, bringing us closer to positive solutions and giving us hope for a bright future.

cloud nine
albacore steak

Named for the happiness I feel because I have been so blessed

1 teaspoon fresh garlic, minced

5 tablespoons soy sauce

½ teaspoon sesame oil

½ teaspoon rice vinegar

pinch shichimi togarashi (Japanese spice blend)*

dash rayu (chili oil)

6¼ ounces sushi-grade yellowfin tuna, raw (five 1¼-ounce steaks)

4 cherry tomatoes, grilled (recipe at right)

½ tablespoon olive oil

7 tablespoons tonkatsu sauce (Japanese steak sauce)*

1 tablespoon fresh parsley, finely chopped

1 tablespoon fresh cilantro, finely chopped

In a medium bowl, whisk together garlic, soy sauce, sesame oil, rice vinegar, shichimi togarashi, and rayu. Add tuna steaks, toss gently to coat, and marinate for 5 minutes.

Heat a medium-sized skillet over high heat, add olive oil, and heat just until smoking. Add the tuna steaks and cook for about 1 minute on each side. (Fish will be about 10% cooked.) Add grilled cherry tomatoes and tonkatsu sauce. Cook for an additional 3 minutes. Transfer to a serving plate. Garnish with chopped parsley and chopped cilantro.

* Available at Asian markets

GRILLED CHERRY TOMATOES

4 cherry tomatoes

¼ teaspoon olive oil

Preheat oven to 425°F. Place tomatoes on a nonstick pan and drizzle with olive oil. Roast for 10 to 15 minutes. Remove from oven and cool slightly.

CHAPTER **12**

APPRECIATION & ANTICIPATION

 "If you can dream it, you can do it."

—*Walt Disney, American film producer, director, and animator*

More than twenty years have gone by since we opened the doors to the first Mikuni. At that time, we stepped into the unknown and trusted in God that this place named for his kingdom would sustain our family. Little did we know that it would be the start of a journey that would plunge us into valleys of extreme hardship and lift us to mountaintops of pure joy.

We took lots of chances and made lots of mistakes, but we never lost sight of my father's vision. Empowered by faith, we continued to move forward in spite of the obstacles. Most important of all, each of us learned and grew from this incredible voyage—and the adventure continues.

THE JOY OF GIVING

"Hole in one!"

I heard the words just as I stepped back from the tee. The setting was the Mikuni Summer Golf Classic, one of our annual fundraising events. My thoughts started racing: *How can that be? I must be better at this game than I thought! Sometimes I really amaze myself!* But then the reality became apparent.

I had sliced the ball so badly that it flew over the pond and over the trees, landing far from its intended target. I was on the first hole of the Granite Bay Golf Course, but my ball landed in the cup on the eleventh hole. My PGA friends were in awe, and I felt pretty special making that impossible shot. So what if that's not what I was supposed to do? It was all part of the exploration!

That's really what this excursion has been about—opening up to the possibilities and sharing the ride. Mikuni has sponsored these golf tournaments since 1995 as a way to give back to the community that supports us, and we have consistently raised one hundred thousand dollars during each event. Through our charitable foundation, we have made donations to a diversity of schools, churches, hospitals, and other nonprofit organizations. I am so happy to be part of it all, and I thank God every day for His benevolence and the opportunity to help others.

THE BLESSINGS OF FAMILY

My son Koki is nearly six-foot-two and weighs more than two hundred pounds. How can that be? It seems as if my wedding was only yesterday, but I have been happily married to Machiko for seventeen years. Two of my kids are in high school, and two are already in junior high. Where does the time go?

Being a father and raising my children has been such a rewarding experience for me. I have taken responsibility for nurturing their spiritual health and encouraging involvement in sports, while my wife has guided them academically. Together, we have taught them to fear God and enjoy life under any and all circumstances.

It is incredible to think that the family of five who arrived in San Francisco in 1985 is now a family of seventeen. My brother, who is the head executive chef of all the Mikuni restaurants, has three boys with his wife, Yuka. My sister is married to Haru, Mikuni's COO, and they have a son and a daughter. We are a close-knit group, and we stand by each other and support each other unconditionally.

As our family has grown, so has our involvement with our church. Every Sunday, my dad preaches, my mom cooks for the congregation, my sister sings, my brother plays piano, and I have the good fortune of being a worship leader and a moderator. Even though the work we do is small, we are delighted to be a part of the kingdom of God—Mikuni.

THE WONDER OF DREAMS

Dreams are free, so there is no reason not to dream big.

As I look to the future and speculate about what it might hold, I am filled with excitement and anticipation. Sushi is gaining in popularity with each passing year, and the prospect of introducing more and more people to it is exhilarating. I am honored to have the support of dedicated employees and high-energy managers who share my enthusiasm and want to take Mikuni to the next level.

The Bible says, "No eye has seen, no ear has heard, no mind has conceived what God has prepared for those who love Him." I believe this with all my heart, and I have faith that He has prepared something for me that exceeds my imagination and my dreams. With his mercy, I will embrace the journey and the abundant possibilities.

The Arai Family: Chiyoh, Koki, Machiko, Taro, Chisay, and Kayji

konnichiwa green tea tiramisu

Named for "hello"...we invite you to enjoy this sweet treat

¼ cup water

¼ cup brandy

3½ tablespoons green tea powder, separated

3 pasteurized egg yolks

½ cup sugar

8 ounces mascarpone cheese

6 ounces cream cheese

1 cup heavy cream

10 ladyfingers

In a small bowl, combine water, brandy, and 1 tablespoon green tea powder. Set aside.

In a medium bowl, whip egg yolks and sugar with a wire whisk until thick and creamy.

In a large bowl, combine mascarpone and cream cheese and mix well. Slowly add egg mixture, stirring until well blended. Stir in 2 tablespoons green tea powder.

With an electric mixer, whip heavy cream until stiff peaks form. With a spatula, gently fold whipped cream into cheese mixture.

To assemble, spoon ¼ cup of cheese mixture into each of five martini glasses. Cut 1 ladyfinger into two pieces to fit, soak in brandy mixture for 5 seconds, and place on top of cheese mixture in each glass. Repeat layering cheese mixture and ladyfingers three times, ending with cheese mixture. Sprinkle remaining green tea powder on top.

Mikuni Locations

Fair Oaks
Historic. Nostalgic. Masterful.

4323 Hazel Avenue
Fair Oaks, CA 95628
916.961.2112

The Mikuni story began modestly in Fair Oaks in 1987, and this original location maintains its distinction as the true heart of the eight restaurants. Here, skilled chefs use their mastery to produce an endless array of lively flavors, appealing colors, and mesmerizing textures, punctuated by lively banter that creates an ambience of welcoming warmth. Loyal patrons return again and again to the place where it all began, drawn to the tradition that consistently delivers culinary excellence and serves as a reminder of Mikuni's early years.

Roseville
Enthusiastic. Eclectic. Creative.

1565 Eureka Road
Roseville, CA 95661
916.797.2112

Mikuni chefs call out the traditional Japanese salutation, Irasshaimase, to everyone who enters the Roseville restaurant. Their exuberant greeting sets the stage for a festive dining experience, as guests are swept up in an atmosphere of unbridled fun and unsurpassed creativity. The perfect setting for large parties and families, it is rarely the same place twice. While the menu features about 100 choices of sushi rolls, there are hundreds more that never make it into print. And if a diner has a particular yen for something special, it will be made to order and presented with a flourish.

Midtown Sacramento

Dazzling. Exhilarating.
Ultra-Cool.

1530 J Street
Sacramento, CA 95814
916.447.2112

This location in the historic East End Lofts building in midtown Sacramento is alive with the flavors of New York and San Francisco. Utterly cosmopolitan, it boasts a vibrancy and energy that generate an irresistible draw. Art is everywhere in this ultra-cool restaurant—from the amazing intricacy of exquisite sushi rolls to the extraordinary beauty of female Japanese warriors whose likenesses adorn the walls. It is truly a place to see and be seen—amidst the bright lights, bold colors, three sushi bars, and the undeniable hum of excitement in the air.

Arden Fair

Fun. Freestyle. Freaky.

1735 Arden Way
Sacramento, CA 95815
916.564.2114

Taro's by Mikuni offers a dining experience that promises a truly unique menu of culinary possibilities. Guests are taken on a senses-stimulating excursion into a world of extraordinary flavors, compelling textures, and visual enchantment. Extending far beyond the realm of Japanese cuisine, the food is designed to please every palate—from the conservative to the adventurous. Anything can happen here—and often does. It is the only Mikuni restaurant that bears my name, and I like to think it's the one that truly reflects my personality.

Elk Grove

Distinctive. Compelling. Exquisite.

8525 Bond Road
Elk Grove, CA 95624
916.714.2112

The fresh, clean beauty of the Elk Grove décor is inspired by the designs of Frank Lloyd Wright, incorporating the architect's trademark use of linear components and uncluttered lines. Extensive use of wood is enhanced by majestic stands of bamboo, creating an atmosphere of East meets West. With two seating options, guests can choose between the inviting warmth of the all-dining room to the sophisticated energy of the dining room/bar combo. Both promise the exceptional sushi and unparalleled dining experience that distinguish all Mikuni restaurants.

Northstar-at-Tahoe

Sensational. Spectacular. Sierra-Inspired.

5001 Northstar Drive, Suite 5101
Truckee, CA 96161
530.562.2188

Set against the glorious backdrop of the majestic Sierra, this restaurant blends fabulous scenery with equally fabulous sushi. Located in the heart of the Northstar-at-Tahoe village, it boasts decor that blends contemporary Asian design with the ambiance of a European ski lodge. The pale wood on the walls is enhanced by custom East-meets-West paintings by artist Terry Flanigan, a variety of Mikuni T-shirts, and an assortment of restaurant awards that we just had to display. Guests can choose between a high-energy experience at the bar and the relaxation of a quiet booth or table.

Denver Region
Majestic. Massive. Magnificent.

8437 Park Meadows Center Dr.
Lone Tree, CO 80124
303.790.2116

Mikuni Park Meadows, our largest restaurant, makes its home in the Rockies. Located in The Vistas at Park Meadows—the Denver area's ultra-hip outdoor lifestyle shopping center—this newest site adds its own brand of culinary excellence to Colorado. In typical Mikuni fashion, the 8400-square-foot space pulses with an eclectic excitement at every turn. Lighted orbs and metallic fish hang from the ceiling, and paintings of samurai warriors and Japanese beauties adorn the walls. The dining experience, true to Mikuni's commitment to quality and adventure, is unparalleled perfection.

Davis
Inviting. Neighborly. Young at Heart.

500 1st Street, Suite 11
Davis, CA 95616
530.756.2111

A cool, urban vibe balances a warm, friendly atmosphere at Mikuni's restaurant in the Davis Commons. Located right in the heart of the downtown area, this hot spot is within easy walking distance of the UC Davis campus. On any given afternoon or evening, you'll find local families, university students, and business professionals enjoying the spectacular sushi and casual ambience—both indoors and on the charming outside patio. The dining experience is enhanced by a full bar, four large-screen HD TVs, and original artwork by UC Davis students.